Let's Prepare for the Grade Eight Intermediate Social Studies Test

Curt Lader
Northport High School
Northport, New York

BARRON'S

Acknowledgments

Illustrations on pages 47, 70, 72, 81, 152, 161, 163, 211, and 215 by Tom Kerr. © Copyright 2001 by Barron's Educational Series, Inc.

Images on pages 55, 57, 58, 102, 224, 226, and 227 reprinted by permission. © Copyright Corbis Images.

All inquiries should be addressed to:
Barron's Educational Series, Inc.
250 Wireless Boulevard
Hauppauge, New York 11788
http://www.barronseduc.com

International Standard Book No. 0-7641-1566-9

International Standard Serial No. 1532-4001
Printed in The United States of America
9 8 7 6 5 4 3

Contents

CHAPTER 4   TEST-TAKING TIPS / 42

CHAPTER 5   GLOSSARY OF TERMS, HISTORICAL DOCUMENTS, AND KEY COURT DECISIONS / 116

MODEL EXAMINATIONS AND ANSWERS / 140

PREFACE

Barron's *Let's Prepare for the Grade Eight Intermediate Social Studies Test* will help students prepare for the statewide exam scheduled for June 2001. Because the book relies on information provided by the New York State Department of Education, it contains many model exam questions and answers based on actual materials used by the Social Studies Division in preparing the actual test. In addition, the author has included his own sample questions and answers. The model examinations at the end of the book include a prototype exam prepared by the New York State Education Department in June 2000 and one developed by Suffolk County's Board of Cooperative Educational Services (BOCES).

Future printings of *Let's Prepare for the Grade Eight Intermediate Social Studies Test* will contain actual exams with easy-to-understand answer sections. These answer sections will include full explanations of all multiple-choice and constructed response questions. Sample student responses to document-based questions, including essays, will also be provided.

This book resembles *Barron's Regents Exams and Answers: U.S. History and Government* both in form and content. One of the reasons why the State Department of Education instituted the Grade Eight Intermediate Social Studies Test was to help prepare and familiarize students with the multiple-choice, constructed response, and document-based questions that they will encounter on Regents exams and in high school social studies classes. Many students rely heavily on Barron's test preparation books for Regents review and preparation. Similar to those books, *Let's Prepare for the Grade Eight Intermediate Social Studies Test* incorporates test-taking tips and provides model questions and answers.

This book strives to make students comfortable with the new question formats and have an easier time adjusting to the rigorous tests taken not only in the eighth grade, but also in tenth and eleventh grades as well.

Chapter 1

What the Exam Is About

You're completing the eighth grade and you're looking forward to entering high school. But before the end of your middle school experience your social studies teacher tells you that every eighth grader in New York State must take the Grade Eight Intermediate Social Studies Test.

This test, just like the fifth grade test that many of your younger brothers and sisters have taken, will contain multiple-choice questions, questions related to historical documents called "constructed response questions," and essays called "document-based questions" (DBQ's). But don't panic. If you have been doing well on your classroom tests all year and you devote some time for review and preparation, you will have no trouble doing well on this exam.

Why do I say this? Because the New York State Department of Education has given your teacher helpful guidelines, and throughout your elementary and intermediate school years, you have been trained in specific skills related to social studies. These skills are called standards. There are five major standards that are emphasized in social studies:

1. United States and New York State History
2. World History
3. Geography
4. Economics
5. Civics, Citizenship, and Government

You have also been taught to use a variety of intellectual skills. These skills involve an understanding of major ideas, eras, themes, developments, and turning points in the history of the United States and New York. So even before you begin to review, you should know a great deal about the material that will be on the test.

For example, you already know how the United States developed its economic system. You have learned how social and political institutions help shape the decisions made in our society. You have been shown how geography impacts the world that we live in. You understand how governments are created and, more specifically, you know about the U.S. system of government under the Constitution.

Taking these general factors into account, the State Department of Education developed an assessment test based on social studies learning standards and performance indicators. These standards are found in *The Social Studies Resource Guide*. Multiple-choice questions, document-based constructed response questions, and document-based essays will be developed based on the material found in the guide. Subject matter includes a chronological history of the United States, from the global heritage of the American people prior to 1500 through citizenship in today's world. The curriculum is split in two parts, with the first part being covered in seventh grade.

Unlike high school, where you must pass Regents exams in order to graduate, the eighth grade test will be used to see how well you are meeting the standards developed by New York State. The test will also serve as a means of providing academic intervention, better known as extra help, if you do poorly. So do the best you can and become familiar with the type of exam you will face when you take the Global History and Geography and U.S. History and Government Regents exams in high school.

THE NATURE OF THE GRADE EIGHT INTERMEDIATE SOCIAL STUDIES TEST

Let's take a look at the specifics of the eighth grade test. You will have a total of three hours to complete the test. Even though there are no specific time guidelines for each section, it is suggested that you follow the general guidelines found on the chart on page 3.

Specifically, in Part I of the Grade Eight Test, you will have to answer 45 multiple-choice questions. You should take about 45 minutes to complete the questions. Part I will be worth 50 percent of your total score.

In Part II of the test you will have to answer questions, based on three to four documents, called "constructed response questions." These documents might be eyewitness accounts, primary sources, diaries, posters, cartoons, graphs, charts, maps, quotes, or short readings. You will have to answer three to four questions related to each document. You should spend about

45 minutes completing the section. It will be worth 20 percent of your score.

The last section of the test is Part III, the document-based question. The document-based question is made up of two parts and will contain six to seven documents. You will have a total of 90 minutes to complete Part III. You should take about 30 to 45 minutes to answer the short answer questions in Part A and use the remainder of the time to write your essay for Part B. The short answer document-based questions are very similar in style to the constructed response questions in Part II of the test. Each of the six to seven documents will have up to four questions called "scaffolding questions." These questions ask you about the information contained in the documents. The short answer type responses are worth approximately 10 percent of your total score. After you finish answering the short answer questions, your last task will be to develop an essay based on historical information given to you and the information you find in the documents. The essay accounts for 20 percent of your score. You will have approximately 45 minutes to complete the Part B essay question.

Some of you may be concerned that you will run out of time, that the questions or documents will be too difficult to understand, or that you won't be able to write an essay based on documents. For this reason, we have included an in-depth review section that breaks the test down section by section and gives you multiple-choice clues, constructed response hints, and document-based question pointers. So, be sure to review "Test-Taking Tips" on pages 42 to 115.

WEIGHTING OF THE GRADE EIGHT INTERMEDIATE SOCIAL STUDIES TEST COMPONENTS

Type of Item	Number of Items	Time	Weight
Multiple-choice	45	45 minutes	50%
Constructed response	3–4	45 minutes	20%
Document-based question	1	90 minutes	30% 10% scaffolding 20% essay
		3 hours	100%

Chapter 2

How to Use This Book

This book will help you review for and take the Grade Eight Intermediate Social Studies Test. It will also let you see how well you have developed the skills you will need for your high school social studies classes.

TEST-TAKING TIPS

Reading the review section of this book should be your first step in getting ready for the test. Each part of the test has its own unique characteristics. And because this test is more complex than the typical one-period classroom test you are familiar with, you should look at the general overview of the test first.

After reviewing the overview of the various test components, you should sharpen your pencil and take note of the specific tips. For the multiple-choice section, you will get clues on how to best answer these questions. Practice the sample questions until you get them right. Note the kind of mistakes you are making in an attempt to get them right the next time.

You will also receive helpful hints for the section of the test that presents you with up to four documents and short questions to answer, called constructed response questions. Like a good detective, you should be able to look at the documents, read and analyze them, and then respond to the questions that are posed to you.

The final section, the document-based question, will contain sample documents related to a specific historical event. These documents may be exciting eyewitness accounts, diaries, political cartoons, maps, graphs, charts, or short readings of primary source documents (first-hand evidence). Each document will have up to four questions related to it and your first task will be to answer these questions. This process is called "scaffolding." Just like a good builder, you will get the materials necessary to build your essay. This book provides pointers to help you develop a solid essay.

SCORING RUBRICS

After mastering the tips, you will learn how the test will be scored. Unlike a straight 100-point exam, this test is initially scored using what is called a "rubric." This is a scale that will be used by your teacher to determine how many points your answer is worth. It applies to the document-based portions of the test. This book provides sample rubrics so that you will better understand what is needed in order to get complete credit for your answers. Scoring rubrics will be used to score the constructed response questions, the document-based questions, and the essay you write.

CHART OF INTERMEDIATE SOCIAL STUDIES MULTIPLE-CHOICE ITEMS

For the multiple-choice section you will see a chart called the "Intermediate Social Studies Multiple-Choice Items." This chart describes the percentage of multiple-choice items that come from a particular unit. It provides you with a range of questions that may be asked for each unit and will help you focus your attention on the subject matter that may be selected for the multiple-choice section of the test.

GRADE EIGHT INTERMEDIATE SOCIAL STUDIES TEST SPECIFICATIONS GRID
Revised (2000)
NUMBER OF MULTIPLE–CHOICE ITEMS BY STANDARD AND UNIT

Standard → / ↓ Unit	1 US and NY History	2 World History	3 Geography	4 Economics	5 Civics, Citizen–ship, and Government	Range
1–Prior to 1500	1–3	0–1	1–3	0–2	0–1	2–4
2–Exploration/Colonization	1–3	0–2	1–3	0–2	0–2	2–5
3–A Nation Created	1–3	0–2	0–2	1–2	1–2	3–5
4–Experiment in Government	1–2	0–1	0–1	0–1	2–4	3–5
5–Life in a New Nation	1–3	0–1	1–2	0–1	0–1	2–4
6–Division and Reunion	1–2	0	1–2	0–2	0–2	2–4
7–An Industrial Society	1–3	0	1–2	1–3	0–1	3–5
8–An Interdependent World	1–3	0–3	0–1	0–1	0–1	2–4
9–Between the Wars	1–3	0–1	0–1	2–4	0–2	3–5
10–Worldwide Responsibilities	2–4	1–2	0–2	0–1	0–2	4–5
11–WW II to the Present	1–2	0–1	0–2	0–2	1–3	2–4
11*–Cross-Topical	1–3	0–2	0–2	0–2	0–2	2–4
Total						45

*Items placed in row 11 are cross-topical. Cross-topical items address content from two or more units.

To get a better feel for the scope and sequence of the material that you should be reviewing, you also have a topic outline arranged in chronological order. This subject outline includes the key topics covered in the seventh and eighth grades based on the standards developed by the New York State Education Department.

Because so much of the exam relies on your ability to understand terminology and analyze information, Chapter 5 of this book provides you with a glossary of key terms and a listing of key documents mentioned in the topic outline. The terms selected are rated using an asterisk (*). One asterisk (*) indicates that the term is found on a test. Two asterisks (**) indicate that the term has been used more than once. The documents selected are also rated, using a plus sign (+). One plus sign (+) indicates that the document is found in the constructed response or the document-based question section of a test. Two plus signs (++) indicate that the document is used in more than one part of an exam.

The final section of the book, Model Examinations and Answers, incorporates all the training, reviewing, and practicing that you have completed. The two exams include a model test based on the author's research in co-operation with Suffolk BOCES and a prototype test developed by the New York State Education Department that was given to students as a sample of what they could expect. These tests have model answers and you should take them more than once. Your goal in doing so should be to identify the types of questions you are getting wrong so that you can review and practice them until you get them right.

A BRIEF RECAP

1. Make sure you understand the nature of the test.
2. Break the test down into its three components—the multiple-choice section (Part I), the constructed response section (Part II), and the document-based question (Part III).
3. Read the directions and information provided for each section of the test.
4. Look over the general description and sample questions for each part of the test.
5. Make a list of the test-taking tips—the multiple-choice clues, the constructed response hints, and the document-based pointers.
6. Understand the scoring rubrics for each part of the test.

7. After you review the chronological topic outline, determine the areas you need to concentrate on.
8. Look at the key terms and recognize those words you are having difficulty with. If you must, make flash cards for review.
9. Answer all model questions as you go along. For any questions you get wrong, go back and answer them again after reviewing the appropriate content areas.
10. And finally, take the model exams under exam conditions. Score the exam using the rubrics provided in the exam.

With practice you will see a steady improvement!

Chapter 3

Chronological Topic Outline of the Seventh and Eighth Grade Curriculum

UNIT ONE: THE GLOBAL HERITAGE OF THE AMERICAN PEOPLE PRIOR TO 1500

I. History and Social Sciences: The Study of People

    A. History and the other social sciences provide a framework and methodology for a systematic study of human cultures.

        1. The role of history and the historian
        2. The other social sciences include anthropology, economics, geography, political science, psychology, and sociology.

    B. The social scientific method as a technique for problem solving and decision making

II. Geographic Factors Influence Culture

    A. Theories attempt to explain human settlement in the Americas.

        1. Anthropologists theorize that Asians migrated across a land bridge between Asia and the Americas.
        2. Native American Indians believe in indigenous development with migration patterns in both directions.

    B. Geographic factors affected the settlement patterns and living conditions of the earliest Americans.

    C. Major Native American civilizations in Central and South America

III. Iroquoian and Algonquian Cultures on the Atlantic Coast of North America

    A. Iroquoian (*Haudenosaunee*—People of the Longhouse) and Algonquian people adapted to the environment in which they settled.

        1. Geographic regions of New York
        2. Diversity of flora and fauna
        3. Seasons and weather patterns
        4. Kinds of settlements and settlement patterns

    B. The Iroquois developed cultural patterns that reflected their needs and values.

        1. Creation and religious beliefs
        2. Importance of the laws of nature and the wise use of natural resources
        3. Patterns of time and space
        4. Family and kinship
        5. Education
        6. Government: Iroquois Confederacy and political organizations at the village level (tribal organization)
        7. Conceptions of land ownership and use
        8. Language

    C. Algonquian Culture

        1. Spiritual beliefs
        2. Spatial patterns

IV. European Conceptions of the World in 1500

    A. European knowledge was based on a variety of sources.

        1. Accounts of early travelers and explorers
        2. A variety of different maps
        3. Writings of ancient scholars
        4. Guesswork
        5. Oral traditions and histories

    B. Different worldviews and ethnocentrism resulted in many misconceptions.

UNIT TWO: EUROPEAN EXPLORATION AND COLONIZATION OF THE AMERICAS

I. European Exploration and Settlement

   A. Motivating factors

      1. Technological improvements in navigation
      2. Consolidation of political power within certain European countries
      3. Desire to break into the eastern trade markets
      4. Missionary zeal

   B. Geographic factors influenced European exploration and settlement in North and South America.

      1. Effects of weather and natural hazards on the Atlantic crossings
      2. Characteristics of different physical environments in the Americas and where different Europeans settled
      3. The development of "New England," "New France," "New Netherlands," and "New Spain"

   C. Effects of exploration and settlement in America and Europe—human-induced changes in the physical environment of the Americas caused changes in other places.

      1. Introduction of new diseases to the Americas was devastating.
      2. The continued growth of population in the colonies resulted in the unjust acquisition of Native American lands.
      3. New types of foods improved both European and Native American health and life spans.
      4. Economic and political changes in the balance of power in Europe and the Americas
      5. Introduction of African slaves into the Americas

   D. Exploration and settlement of New York State area by the Dutch and English.

      1. Relationships between the colonists and the Native American Indians
      2. Similarities between the Europeans and Native American Indians

      a. The role of tradition

      b. The importance of families and kinship ties

      c. The hierarchical nature of the community and family

      d. The need to be self-sufficient

   3. Differences

      a. Ideas about land ownership

      b. Roles of men and women

      c. Beliefs about how people from different cultures should be addressed

   4. Rivalry between the Dutch and English eventually resulted in English supremacy.

II. Colonial Settlement: Geographic, Political, and Economic Factors

  A. English colonies: New England, Middle Atlantic, Southern

    1. Reviewed as a geographic region—criteria to define regions, types of regions

    2. Settlement patterns: Who? When? Why?

    3. Economic patterns emerge to meet diverse needs: agricultural and urban settlements.

    4. Political systems: the Mayflower Compact

    5. Social order

  B. French and Spanish colonies

    1. Reviewed as a geographic region—types, connections between regions

    2. Settlement patterns: Who? When? Why?

    3. Economic patterns emerge to meet diverse needs.

    4. Political systems and social order

III. Life in Colonial Communities

  A. Colonial communities were the center of social, economic, and political life and tended to develop along European patterns.

    1. Variations were found.

      a. Religious-based

      b. Slave and free black communities

      c. Place of national origin

2. The social structure promoted interdependence.
3. Social goals promoted community consciousness over individual rights.
4. Role of religions
   a. Puritans
   b. Quakers
   c. Catholics
   d. Others
5. Survival demanded cooperation and a strong work ethic.
6. Importance of waterways
7. A hierarchical social order created social inequity.

B. Structure and roles of colonial families

1. Nuclear families made up the basic social and economic unit.
2. Authority and obligation followed kinship lines.
3. Roles of family members

C. Life in colonial communities was a reflection of geographic and social conditions.

1. Impact of physical environments
   a. Travel
   b. Communication
   c. Settlements
   d. Resource use
2. Social conditions led to
   a. Different forms of government
   b. Varying roles of religion
   c. Inequalities of economic conditions
   d. Unequal treatment of blacks
3. The impact of geographic and social conditions could be seen in the divergent landholding systems that developed in:
   a. New England
   b. New Netherlands: patroonship system
   c. Southern colonies: plantation system
4. Life in French and Spanish colonies was both similar to and different from life in other colonies.

UNIT THREE: A NATION IS CREATED

I. Background Causes of the American Revolution

    A. Economic factors

        1. Growth of mercantilism: triangular trade
        2. Rise of an influential business community in the colonies
        3. Cost of colonial wars against the French

    B. Political factors

        1. The role of the British Civil War
        2. Periods of political freedom in the colonies
        3. Impact of the French and Indian War: Albany Plan of Union
        4. Political thought of the Enlightenment influenced prominent colonial leaders

    C. New social relationships between European powers and the American colonies: development of a new colonial identity

II. The Shift from Protest to Separation

    A. New British attitude toward colonies following victory over France.

        1. Colonies could not protect themselves.
        2. Colonies were not paying a fair amount toward their support.

    B. New British policies antagonized many American colonists.

        1. Various acts of Parliament such as the Quebec Act
        2. New tax policies and taxes: Stamp Act and others
        3. Other acts of repression: *Zenger* case and others

    C. Public opinion was shaped in different forums.

        1. Political bodies
        2. Public display and demonstration
        3. Print media

    D. Wide variety of viewpoints evolved.

        1. Complete separation
        2. More autonomy for the colonies
        3. No change in status quo: the Loyalist position

III. Early Attempts to Govern the Newly Independent States

    A. The Revolution begins.

        1. Early confrontations
        2. Important leaders
        3. First Continental Congress

    B. The Second Continental Congress represented the first attempt to govern the colonies.

        1. Republican government
        2. Request for state constitutions and political systems
        3. Asserting independence

    C. A movement for independence evolved from the political debate of the day.

    D. Declaration of Independence

        1. Origins
        2. Content
        3. Impact
        4. Ideals embodied

    E. Independence creates problems for New Yorkers.

        1. Organizing new state government
        2. Economic problems
        3. Political factions
        4. Slavery
        5. Recruiting soldiers for the war

IV. Military and Political Aspects of the Revolution

    A. Strategies of the principal military engagements

        1. Washington's leadership
        2. New York as the object of strategic planning
        3. Evolution of the war from the North to the South: Lexington and Concord to Saratoga and Yorktown

    B. Role of the Loyalists

        1. In New York City
        2. Colonists in Nova Scotia, Quebec, and Prince Edward Island did not join the Revolution.
            a. Refuge for Loyalists
            b. Staging ground for attacks on New York patriots

    C. The outcome of the war was influenced by many factors.

        1. Personalities and leadership
        2. Geography: importance of various physical features
        3. Allocation of resources
        4. Foreign aid: funds and volunteers
        5. Role of women, blacks, and Native American Indians
        6. Haphazard occurrences of events: the human factor
        7. Clash between colonial authority and Second Continental Congress

V. Economic, Political, and Social Changes Brought About by the American Revolution

    A. On the national level

        1. Britain gave up claims to govern.
        2. Slavery began to emerge as a divisive sectional issue because slaves did not receive their independence.
        3. American economy was plagued by inflation and hurt by isolation from world markets.

    B. In New York State

        1. The effects of the American Revolution on the Iroquois Confederacy
        2. Disposition of Loyalist property and resettlement of many Loyalists after the Revolution to Canada, thus changing the French/British balance
        3. A republican ideology developed that emphasized shared power and citizenship participation.

C. In the Western Hemisphere

1. Britain did not accept the notion of American dominance of the hemisphere.
2. The remaining British colonies in Canada strengthened their ties to Great Britain.
3. Many leaders in South America drew inspiration from American ideas and actions in their struggle against Spanish rule.

UNIT FOUR: EXPERIMENTS IN GOVERNMENT

I. The Articles of Confederation and the Critical Period

A. Need for a formal plan of union

1. Historical precedent: the Albany Plan of Union
2. Development of state constitutions
3. Inadequacy of Continental Congress as a national government

B. Development of a formal plan of government

1. Draft and debate in Congress (1776–1777)
2. Ratification by the states (1778–1781)
   a. Period of operation (1781–1789)

C. The structure of government under the Articles of Confederation

1. Congress was the only branch of government.
2. Each state had equal representation.
3. Congressional power under the Articles included:
   a. Making war and peace
   b. Conducting foreign and Native American Indian affairs
   c. The settlement of disputes between and among states
   d. Issuance of currency and borrowing

D. The Articles suffered from many weaknesses.

1. Indirect representation
2. No coercive power; decisions more advisory than binding (for example, Shays' Rebellion)
3. Lack of national executive and judicial functions
4. Lack of taxing power
5. Difficulty in passing legislation

E. The Articles did have several achievements and contributions.

  1. The Land Ordinance of 1785 and the Northwest Ordinance (1787)
  2. Developed the privileges and immunities of citizenship
  3. Developed the concept of limited government

II. The New York State Constitution of 1777

  A. Adopted by convention without submission to popular vote

    1. Included Declaration of Independence
    2. Influence of leaders such as John Jay

  B. Chronology of the document

    1. Draft and debate in convention (1776–1777)
    2. Period of operation (1777–1822)

  C. Form of early state government

    1. Similar to colonial government
    2. Governor with limited authority and three-year term
    3. Inclusion of rights and liberties
    4. First system of state courts
    5. Limited franchise
    6. Bicameral legislature: Senate (four-year term); Assembly (one-year term)

  D. Effectiveness

    1. Smoother functioning than national government under the Articles of Confederation
    2. Cumbersome administrative procedures
    3. Excessive use of veto procedures
    4. A model for the United States Constitution of 1787

III. The Writing, Structure, and Adoption of the United States Constitution

  A. Annapolis Convention (1786)

    1. Impracticality of correcting weaknesses in Articles of Confederation

    2. Need for an improved form of government without losing key elements of a new philosophy of government

    3. Decision to write a constitution

B. Constitutional Convention: setting and composition

C. Major issues

    1. Limits of power: national versus state

    2. Representation: slaves and apportionment

    3. Electoral procedures: direct versus indirect election

    4. Rights of individuals

D. The need for compromise

    1. The issue of a federal or a national government

    2. The Great Compromise on representation

    3. The Three-Fifths Compromise on slavery

    4. The commerce compromises

E. The underlying legal and political principles of the Constitution

    1. Federalism

    2. Separation of powers

    3. Provisions for change

    4. Protection of individual rights

F. The Constitution and the functioning of the federal government

    1. The Preamble states the purpose of the document

    2. The structure and function of the legislative, executive, and judicial branches (Articles I, II, and III)

    3. The relation of states to the federal union (Article IV)

    4. Assuming the responsibility for a federal system (Article VI)

G. The Constitution as a "living" document

    1. The elastic clause and delegated power facilitate action.

    2. Amendment procedure as a mechanism for change (Article V)

    3. The Bill of Rights

    4. Supreme Court decisions

H. The evolution of an "unwritten constitution"

    1. Political parties

    2. The president's cabinet

3. President's relation to Congress
4. Committee system in Congress
5. Traditional limitations on presidential term

I. The ratification process

1. The debates in the states, especially New York State
2. The Federalist Papers
3. Poughkeepsie Convention
   a. Federalists (Hamilton)
   b. Anti-federalists (Clinton)
4. Formal ratification of the Constitution and launching of the new government
5. The personal leadership of people such as Washington, Franklin, Hamilton, and Madison

UNIT FIVE: LIFE IN THE NEW NATION

I. New Government in Operation

A. Washington as president: precedents

B. Establishing stability

1. Hamilton's economic plan
2. The Whiskey Rebellion
3. Preserving neutrality: the French Revolution, Citizen Genêt, Jay, and Pinckney Treaties
4. Political parties
5. Election of 1800
6. Judicial review: *Marbury* v. *Madison* (1803)

C. Expanding the nation's boundaries

1. Pinckney Treaty with Spain
2. Louisiana Purchase
3. War of 1812: guaranteeing boundaries
4. Monroe Doctrine: sphere of influence
5. Purchase of Florida
6. Native American Indian concessions and treaties

D. Challenges to stability

    1. French and English trade barriers and the Embargo Act
    2. War of 1812: second war for independence

E. The Era of Good Feelings

    1. Clay's American system
    2. Internal expansion: new roads, canals, and railroads
    3. Protective tariffs
    4. National assertions: Marshall's decision (*Gibbons* v. *Ogden*, 1824)
    5. Extension of slavery by the Missouri Compromise
    6. Threats to Latin America: the Monroe Doctrine
    7. Disputed election of 1824

II. The Age of Jackson

A. The age of the "common man"

    1. Expansion of suffrage
    2. Citizenship
    3. Election of 1828
    4. Jackson: man, politician, and president
    5. The "spoils system"
    6. New political parties

B. Jackson's Native American policy reflected frontier attitudes.

    1. Some Native Americans resisted government attempts to negotiate their removal by treaty.
    2. Government policy of forced removals (1820–1840) resulted in widespread suffering and death.
    3. Native American Indian territory

C. Intensifying sectional differences

    1. Protective tariff (1828)
    2. Nullification controversy (1828, 1832)
    3. Clay's compromise tariff (1833)

III. Pre-industrial Age: 1790–1860s

   A. Portrait of the United States (1800)

      1. Agriculturally based economy
      2. Urban centers on the coast
      3. Poor communication and transportation systems
      4. Self-sufficiency
      5. Regional differences

   B. Patterns of community organization, work, and family life in agrarian America

   C. Technological changes altered the way people dealt with one another.

      1. Improved transportation made travel and communication easier.
      2. Greater ties between communities were possible.
      3. The Erie Canal and its impact
         a. Reasons for building the Erie Canal
         b. Technology involved in its construction
         c. Types and sources of labor: ethnic and racial labor force
         d. Results of building the Erie Canal

   D. The impact of early industrialization and technological changes on work and workers, the family, and the community

      1. An increase in the production of goods for sale rather than personal use
      2. Increased purchasing of what was formerly produced at home
      3. Emergence of a new work ethic

   E. Family roles changed, affecting society in general.

      1. Changing role of women
      2. Childhood became a more distinct stage of life.
      3. Roles of private agencies

   F. Slavery and Abolition

      1. Review of the institution of slavery
      2. The meaning and morality of slavery
      3. Abolition movement

      a. Leadership (Tubman, Garrison, and others)

      b. Activities (for example, Freedom Trail and the Underground Railroad)

  4. Abolition in New York State

  5. Canada's role

  6. Effects of Abolition

G. Social changes

  1. Religious revival

  2. Women's rights

  3. Mental hospital and prison reform

  4. Education

  5. Temperance

H. An American culture begins to emerge.

  1. Literature

  2. Art

I. Portrait of the United States (1860)

  1. Growth brought about many changes and regions—the spatial patterns of settlement in different regions in the United States

      a. The size and shape of communities.

      b. Environmental impacts due to development of natural resources and industry—human modification of the physical environment

      c. The diversity of people within the larger communities and regions

      d. The ability of the political system within communities to deal with deviance

      e. The Pre-industrial Age took place at different times in different places

  2. The North

      a. Industrial base

      b. Increasing population

      c. Urban-centered—"causes and consequences of urbanization"

  3. The South

      a. Agricultural base (cotton)

      b. Impact of Industrial Revolution on agriculture

      c. Increasing slave population

UNIT SIX: DIVISION AND REUNION

I. Underlying Causes of the Civil War

   A. Territorial expansion and slavery

   1. The secession of Texas (1836)
   2. The Mexican War (1846–1848)
   3. Oregon Territory
   4. The westward movement and its effects on the physical, social, and cultural environments

   B. The emotional impact of slavery

   1. *Uncle Tom's Cabin*
   2. John Brown's raid on Harper's Ferry
   3. Fugitive slave laws

   C. Failure of political compromise

   1. Compromise of 1850
   2. Kansas-Nebraska Act (1854)
   3. Founding of the Republican Party (1854–1856)
   4. *Dred Scott* v. *Sanford* (1857)
   5. Lincoln-Douglas debate (1858)
   6. Election of 1860
   7. Firing on Fort Sumter (1861)

II. The Civil War Begins

   A. The presidency of Lincoln

   1. Personal leadership
   2. Opposition
   3. Emancipation Proclamation

   B. Advantages and disadvantages of each side

   1. Advantages
      a. South
         i. Military leadership
         ii. Commitment of people to preserve their way of life

        b. North
- **i.** Effective navy
- **ii.** Larger army
- **iii.** Manufacturing
- **iv.** Agricultural production
- **v.** Transportation system

  2. Disadvantages
      a. South
- **i.** Lacked manufacturing
- **ii.** Lacked a navy
- **iii.** Not prepared for war

      b. North
- **i.** Lacked quality military leadership
- **ii.** Not prepared for war

      c. The military and political dimensions of the war

  3. Geographic factors influenced the war's progress and outcome—role of physical and other barriers

  4. Major campaigns evolved around a changing strategy on both sides.

  5. Wartime problems and political issues

  6. Foreign policy maneuvering was crucial to the final outcome.
      a. Seward's concern with Mexico
      b. Emancipation Proclamation as an element of foreign policy

  7. Technology of the war

C. New York State in the Civil War

  1. Military role
  2. Political opposition in New York City
  3. Conscription laws and draft riots
      a. Undemocratic nature of the draft
      b. Conscription as a factor in racism

III. Results of the Civil War

A. Preservation of the Union

B. Abolition of slavery

  1. The Emancipation Proclamation.
  2. Civil Rights and the Thirteenth Amendment.

C. Political power and decision making

   1. Secession
   2. States' rights

D. Reconstruction—theory, practice, and termination

   1. Lincoln's plan
   2. Johnson's plan and Congressional opposition resulted in his impeachment.
   3. Congressional Reconstruction
   4. Constitutional Amendments 14 and 15 guarantee equal rights for all races except Native American Indians.
   5. Problems of economic and social reconstruction led to sharecropping as a substitute for slavery.
   6. The official end of Reconstruction in 1877
   7. Segregation held legal: *Plessy* v. *Ferguson* (1896)

E. The enormous human suffering and loss of life caused by the war

UNIT SEVEN: AN INDUSTRIAL SOCIETY

I. The Maturing of an Industrial Society in the Second Half of the Nineteenth Century

A. Problems and progress in American politics: Framework for a changing United States

   1. New problems created a changing role for government and the political system.
   2. Scandals, depressions, and limitations of traditional politics resulted in reluctant change (for example, civil service)
   3. National politics were dominated by the Democratic and Republican parties, but third parties occasionally arose to meet special interests.
   4. New York State and New York City in an era of machine politics (for example, the Tweed Ring and Tammany Hall)
   5. Prevailing attitude of non-interference (*laissez-faire*) as the appropriate role for government, with some regulations to meet excesses

B. The United States developed as an industrial power.

1. Changes in the methods of production and distribution of manufactured goods
   a. Transportation developments and their effects on economic developments (1865–1900)
   b. Communication developments (1865–1900)
   c. Industrial technology (1865–1900)
   d. Rise of banking and financial institutions
2. Increase in the number and size of firms engaged in manufacture and distribution of goods
3. Increase in the number and skill level of workers; new labor markets
4. Expansion of markets for manufactured goods
5. The growth and emerging problems of the cities

C. Growth of the corporation as a form of business organization: Case studies—oil, railroads, and steel

1. One of several forms of business organization
2. Many firms maintained traditional ways of doing business.
3. Advantages and disadvantages of a corporation

D. Government response to industrial development and abuses

1. *Laissez-faire* versus regulation
2. Interstate commerce: state and national control
3. Sherman Anti-trust Act: bigness as a threat

E. Changing patterns of agricultural organization and activity in the United States and New York State

1. Unprecedented growth in agriculture
2. Changes in the methods of production and distribution of farm products—spatial distribution of economic activities
3. Efficient use of resources combined with competition and the profit motive to improve methods of production.

F. Occurrence of many significant and influential changes

1. Communities grew in size and number.
2. Interdependence increased.

3. Decision-making procedures changed.
4. Technology advanced.
5. Adaptation of, rather than to, the environment—human modifications of the physical environment
6. Perceptions of time became more formal (for example, railroad schedules).
7. Political machines influenced daily life.

G. The response of labor to industrialization

1. Industrialization created a larger workforce and more complex work.
2. Working conditions underwent extensive change, which often placed hardships on workers; roles of women, children, minorities, and disabled persons changed.
3. Early attempts to unionize the workforce met with resistance and failure (for example, the Knights of Labor and the Haymarket Riot, American Railway Union, the Industrial Workers of the World).
4. Roots of modern labor unionism (for example, the American Federation of Labor)
5. Labor as a reform movement in other aspects of society

H. The response of the farmer to industrialization

1. Expanding agricultural production and railroads
2. Cheap money and high railroad rates
3. The Grange and state reforms
4. The Populist movement
5. The closing of the frontier—limitations of physical environment

II. Changes in the Social Structure Altered the American Scene.

A. The immigration experience

1. Two distinct waves occurred, from the 1840s to the 1890s, and from the 1890s to the early 1920s; migration streams over time.
2. Differences were based on national origins, cultural patterns, and religion.
3. Similarities included motivations for coming and patterns of community settlement.

4. Initial clashes ended in varying degrees of acculturation.
5. Occupational and political experiences varied.

B. Case studies of the immigrant experience in the United States and New York State—population characteristics

1. A comparison of European immigrants and the black slave experience—human migration's effects on the character of different places and regions
2. Immigrants as rural settlers in the Midwest
3. The Chinese experience in the Far West
4. Mexicans in the Southwest
5. New York City's ethnic neighborhoods
6. French-Canadian settlement in northern New York State
7. Immigration patterns and experiences throughout New York State
8. Irish immigration: mass starvation in Ireland (1845–1850)
9. Immigrants in the local community

C. Legal basis for citizenship in the United States

1. Citizenship by the "law of the soil"
2. Citizenship by birth to an American parent
3. Citizenship through naturalization

D. Responsibilities of citizenship

1. Civic: A citizen should be:
   a. knowledgeable about the process of government.
   b. informed about major issues.
   c. a participant in the political process.
2. Legal: A citizen should:
   a. be knowledgeable about the law.
   b. obey the laws.
   c. respect the rights of others.
   d. understand the importance of law in a democratic society.
3. The changing role of the citizen

E. America becomes an increasingly mobile society.

1. Motivated by new economic opportunities
2. Changing patterns of movement (for example, blacks begin to move North)

3. Westward settlement
4. The disappearance of the frontier—physical limits of geography

F. America developed as a consumer society.

1. Improved standard of living increased consumption.
2. Greater variety of goods available
3. Continually rising expectations

G. Leisure activities reflected the prevailing attitudes and views of the time

1. Greater variety of leisure activities became available as less time was spent on work.
2. Leisure activities reflected general characteristics of modern society (i.e., organized use of technology, emphasis on the individual role, and reliance on experts).

III. The Progressive Movement (1900–1920): Efforts to Reform the New Society

A. Social ills

1. The muckrakers—exposing corruption and abuses in industry, government, and urban living conditions
2. Fighting racial discrimination (for example, the formation of the NAACP)
3. Temperance and Prohibition
4. Settlement houses

B. Efforts to reform government and politics

1. Need for responsive government (for example, primary elections, the initiative, the referendum, and the recall election)
2. Progressive leaders, (for example, LaFollette, Theodore Roosevelt, Taft, and Debs)
3. The Socialist Party challenges the political establishment.
4. Direct election of Senators—the Seventeenth Amendment
5. Women's suffrage—the Nineteenth Amendment

C. Economic reform efforts.

1. Labor-related legislation (for example, minimum wage laws, workmen's compensation insurance, safety regulations, and child labor laws)
2. Prosecuting trusts
3. Government regulation of the railroads
4. The Federal Reserve Act
5. Graduated income tax—the Sixteenth Amendment

UNIT EIGHT: THE UNITED STATES AS AN INDEPENDENT NATION IN AN INCREASINGLY INTERDEPENDENT WORLD

I. The United States Expands Its Territories and Builds an Overseas Empire

A. Growth of imperialist sentiment was caused by several factors.

1. A belief that the nation had a right to the land (i.e., Manifest Destiny—"people's differing perceptions of places, people, and resources")
2. Perceived moral obligations to extend America's way of life to others (ethnocentrism and racism)
3. American citizens were already migrating into new lands in North America—the effects of human migration on the characteristics of different places.
4. Increased foreign trade led to a growing interest in gaining control of some foreign markets.
5. Fear that foreign nations would gain control of strategic locations at the expense of the United States
6. Developing technology in transportation and communication contributed to American expansion potential—the importance of location and certain physical features.

B. The Spanish-American War signaled the emergence of the United States as a world power.

1. The war's origins lay in Cuban attempts to gain freedom from Spain.

2. Concerns of the United States (pro-expansionist sentiment, Cuba's location, and Spanish tactics)
3. Newspapers shaped public opinion over the *Maine* incident—"yellow journalism."
4. Conduct of the war created domestic and international problems.
5. Opposition to American imperialist movement

C. Victory in the Spanish-American War created a need for a new foreign policy.

1. Acquisition of land far from America's shores—importance of resources and markets
2. Emphasis on doing what the government felt was necessary and possible to protect American interests (maintaining a strong navy, gaining control of strategic locations, advocating equal trading rights in Asia [Open Door Policy])
3. Actions created conflict with Filipinos and Japanese.

D. United States policies in Latin America

1. The United States attempted to control a number of locations in Latin America for economic and political reasons.
2. The quest for Latin American stability through the Roosevelt Corollary to the Monroe Doctrine (the Panama Canal)
3. Armed intervention in Latin America

II. The United States Begins to Take a Role in Global Politics.

A. United States policy on noninvolvement in European political affairs was based on a number of factors.

1. Tradition dating back to the earliest days of the country
2. Focus on the international problems of the new nation
3. Recognition of United States military unpreparedness
4. Impacts of geography (for example, location, resources) on United States foreign policy

B. Pre-World War I involvements

1. Application of the Monroe Doctrine to the Western Hemisphere
2. Threats to American foreign trade
3. Roosevelt's Treaty of Portsmouth

C. World War I occurred as a result of international problems.

   1. Intense nationalism
   2. Power struggles among European nations
   3. A failure of leadership
   4. European alliances

D. Events led to United States' involvement in World War I.

   1. The American people were divided in ways that made involvement difficult.
   2. Fear that United States' involvement would increase intolerance at home
   3. Initial attempts to follow traditional policy of neutrality failed.
   4. Unwillingness of warring nations to accept President Wilson as a mediator
   5. England was a major United States trade partner.
   6. Despite varied ethnic backgrounds in the United States, leaders felt closer to the English than to the Germans.
   7. While both sides attempted to restrict United States trade with their opponent, Germany did so by sinking American ships.
   8. Recognition that the United States would have no say at any peace conference if it remained neutral.

E. The United States entered the war.

   1. Combining new technology with old strategies (chemical warfare led to the death of millions)
   2. The war was supported by the majority of Americans.
   3. The war effort created changes on the home front (for example, economic controls, the role of women in the workforce, black migrations to the North, and attempts to organize labor to improve conditions).
   4. War promoted intolerance (for example, the Espionage Act of 1917 and the Sedition Act of 1918); "hyphenated-Americans" have their loyalty questioned.

F. The United States and the peace negotiations

   1. Wilson's failed attempts to establish leadership with his Fourteen Points

    2. Senate opposition to the League of Nations
    3. The Versailles Treaty

G. The Bolshevik Revolution

    1. Effect of World War I
    2. Civil war in Russia
    3. Western intervention
    4. Threat of international communism

UNIT NINE: THE UNITED STATES BETWEEN THE WARS

I. The Roaring Twenties Reflected the Spirit of the Postwar Period

A. Prohibition and the Eighteenth Amendment

    1. End of reform era
    2. The rise of organized crime
    3. Economic, social, political effects

B. The Republican decade

    1. Political developments
        a. Return to "normalcy"; the election of 1920
        b. Scandals
        c. Coolidge: austerity and integrity
        d. Government and business: *laissez-faire* and protection
        e. Election of 1928

C. Relative isolation of the United States in world political affairs

    1. General policy of noninvolvement in European affairs; the League of Nations controversy
    2. Limited participation in international activities
        a. World Court
        b. Naval disarmament (1924)
        c. Efforts for peace; Kellogg-Briand Pact (1928)
        d. Postwar reparation talks
        e. Relief efforts in Europe
    3. Expansion of international trade and tariffs
    4. Restrictions on immigration (Quota Act, 1924)

D. A rising standard of living resulted in the growth of a consumer economy and the rise of the middle class.

1. Increase in single-family homes; move to nuclear families
2. Emergence of suburbs
3. Spread of middle-class values
4. Increased use of credit

E. Changes in the workplace

1. Shift from agrarian to industrial workforce
2. Lessened demand for skilled workers
3. Working conditions and wages improved.
4. Increase in white-collar employees
5. Women continued to increase their presence in the workforce.

F. Problems developed in the midst of unprecedented prosperity.

1. Not all groups benefited equally.
   a. Low farm prices
   b. High black unemployment
   c. Millions of poor
2. New trends conflicted with tradition.
3. Environmental balance was jeopardized.

G. Foreign immigration and black migration resulted in a very diverse population and an increase in social tensions—the effects of human migration on the nature and character of places and regions.

1. Restrictions on immigration
2. Black migration to Northern cities
3. Growth of organizations to fight discrimination (for example, NAACP)
4. Growth of black art, music, and cultural identity (for example, the Harlem Renaissance)
5. Generational conflicts
6. Widespread emergence of retired workers
7. Right-wing hate groups

H. New ideas about the use of leisure time emerged.

1. Impact of the automobile: Henry Ford
2. Organized sports: Babe Ruth

3. Search for heroes and heroines: Charles Lindbergh and Amelia Earhart
4. Motion pictures
5. Popular literature
6. Fads and fashion
7. Changes in social behavior

I. The stock market crash marked the beginning of one of the worst economic times the country has ever known.

1. National prosperity had been structured on the investments of the wealthy.
2. There were problems with the economic structure.
3. People lost faith in the system.
4. The government was unwilling or unable to correct the downturn.
5. The economic depression that followed was the worst in our history.

II. The Great Depression

A. Contributing factors

1. Economic growth declined during the late 1920s.
2. Stock purchases were made on margin (credit).
3. Corporations and individuals became over-extended.
4. The stock market crash led to a cycle of low demand and high unemployment.

B. Responses to deepening economic woes

1. Hoover administration response: too little, too late
2. Local and state actions
   a. Soup kitchens and outstretched hands
   b. A modified "New Deal" in New York
3. Election of 1932; question of confidence

C. The New Deal

1. Psychological boost; Franklin Roosevelt at the fireside
2. Relieving human suffering; providing for dignity and jobs
3. Helping business and industry recover
4. Adjusting the economic system to prevent recurrence

     a. Government regulation of business and banking

     b. Instituting Social Security

     c. Providing a guaranteed labor voice: the Wagner Act

  5. Other voices

     a. Court-packing scheme

     b. Alternative solutions: Father Coughlin, the Townsend Plan, Huey Long, socialism, and communism

  6. The economics of war versus depression conditions; climbing out of Depression and into war Spain, Japan; intensified communism characterized by:

     a. One-party governments headed by a strong individual

     b. Armies and police forces fostered national goals and eliminated opposition

     c. Use of propaganda in the media and schools to support national goals

     d. Art and literature were used to endorse official policies in totalitarian countries.

D. European conflicts resulted in several basic problems for United States policy makers.

  1. The question of whether to shift focus from domestic problems to foreign policy

  2. Issue of neutrality versus the growing power of totalitarian states

  3. Continued efforts to improve Latin American relations through the "Good Neighbor Policy" without losing influence in that area's affairs

UNIT TEN: THE UNITED STATES ASSUMES WORLDWIDE RESPONSIBILITIES

I. World War II

  A. Origins of the war

    1. The Versailles Treaty

    2. The Great Depression

    3. Rise of totalitarianism; expansionism and persecution

    4. The rearming of Germany

    5. Isolationism
    6. Failure of the League of Nations

B. Pre-war alliances

    1. Axis powers
    2. Allied powers
    3. Role of the United States

C. Failure of peace

    1. Aggression in Europe (Germany and Italy), Africa (Italy), and Asia (Japan)
    2. Appeasement (Chamberlain in Munich)
    3. German attack on Poland; World War II begins
    4. United States role to 1941—guarded isolation, aid to Allies

D. The United States in World War II

    1. Japanese attack on Pearl Harbor
    2. A two-front war
       a. Europe—Eisenhower
       b. Pacific—MacArthur

E. New aspects of the war

    1. German *blitzkrieg*
    2. Aerial bombing
    3. New technology and its impact on people and the physical environment
    4. Atomic bomb—the Manhattan Project
    5. The Nazi Holocaust
    6. Concept of unconditional surrender

F. The home front

    1. Total mobilization of resources
    2. Rationing
    3. Role of women
    4. War bonds
    5. Internment and incarceration of Japanese-Americans
    6. Limited progress toward economic, political, and social equality for black Americans (Roosevelt's Executive Order 8802)

G. End of the war

    1. Allied agreement—Yalta Conference
    2. Defeat of Germany
    3. Defeat of Japan

H. Impact of the war

    1. Entire countries were physically and demographically devastated—effects of physical and human geographic factors.
    2. Millions of families suffered the loss of loved ones.
    3. The Nazi Holocaust—Hitler's "Final Solution"; worldwide horror; human rights violations
    4. United States response to the Holocaust: Fort Ontario; Oswego, New York
    5. The Nuremberg Trials
    6. Global impact; rise of nationalism in Africa and Asia
    7. Advent of the United Nations
    8. Advent of the nuclear age

II. The United States as Leader of the Free World

A. Role of the United Nations

    1. Human rights issues; United Nations Universal Declaration of Human Rights (1948)—role of Eleanor Roosevelt on the United Nations Commission for Human Rights
    2. Actions of the United Nations to promote peace

B. United States and the Soviet Union emerge as world leaders.

    1. The Cold War
    2. Truman Doctrine and Marshall Plan
    3. Alliance systems (NATO and Warsaw Pact)

C. Communist expansion leads to United States policy of containment.

    1. In Europe: Berlin airlift, Berlin Wall
    2. In Asia: Communist China, Korean War
    3. In Latin America: Cuban missile crisis
    4. In Southeast Asia: Vietnam War

D. Superpower rivalry

  1. The spread of nuclear weapons
  2. The arms race
  3. From *Sputnik* to astronauts on the moon

III. The United States in the Post-Cold War World

  A. Shifting foreign policies help lead to the end of the Cold War.

   1. Détente and arms control beginning with President Nixon
   2. Military build-up and treaties to bring about reductions
   3. Fall of the Berlin Wall (1989) and the collapse of the Soviet Union

  B. The United States seeks a new role in the world.

   1. Arab-Israeli conflicts; Camp David Accord
   2. Persian Gulf War
   3. Peacekeeping missions; Somalia, Bosnia

  C. Western Hemisphere relations

   1. Economic competition and cooperation: NAFTA
   2. Immigration patterns between the United States and Mexico, and Latin America
   3. Spread of democratic principles in Latin America

UNIT ELEVEN: THE CHANGING NATURE OF THE AMERICAN PEOPLE FROM WORLD WAR II TO THE PRESENT

I. Postwar Society Characterized by Prosperity and Optimism

  A. Changing patterns of production and consumption resulting in economic expansion

   1. Increased productivity, a result of improving technology and rising consumer demand, leading to higher wages and declining unemployment
   2. Number of service jobs and women in the workforce increasing
   3. Poverty continues to exist in the midst of plenty.

B. Families and communities undergo significant changes.

    1. Post-war baby boom has major effects on social and economic decisions made by families.
    2. Growth of suburbs parallel movement from major cities.
    3. Effect of automobiles reflected in interstate highway system, shopping centers, and increased commuting to work.

C. Civil rights movement places focus on equality and democracy.

    1. Important executive and judicial decisions support equal rights.
    2. *Brown* v. *Board of Education of Topeka* (1954) overturned legal basis of segregation.
    3. Activists and leaders such as Dr. Martin Luther King, Jr. developed strategies to secure civil rights for African-Americans.
    4. Women, Native Americans, and others also sought greater equality.
    5. Supreme Court moved to protect individual rights: *Miranda* v. *Arizona* (1966), *Tinker* v. *Des Moines Independent School District* (1969).

D. Self-confidence of early post-war years eroded by series of events

    1. Assassinations of major leaders: Kennedy, King, Jr.
    2. Nation split over involvement in Vietnam War
    3. Groups in society turn to violence to reach their goals.
    4. Resignation of President Nixon
    5. Oil crisis and skyrocketing inflation

II. The United States Begins a New Century

A. The United States competes in a world economy.

    1. Competition from Europe, Asia, rest of Western Hemisphere
    2. Effects on economy of the United States

B. Federal and state governments reevaluate their roles.

    1. Fiscal and monetary policies: taxation, regulation, and deregulation
    2. Social programs: health, welfare, and education

C. Technological changes: the home and the workplace

D. Old and new problems must be addressed.

1. Violent crime and substance abuse
2. Protection of the environment
3. Growing number of elderly Americans
4. The continuing struggle for economic and social justice for all citizens
5. Balancing the ideals of national unity with growing cultural diversity
6. Civic and legal responsibilities of citizenship

Chapter 4

Test-Taking Tips

OVERVIEW OF PART I: MULTIPLE-CHOICE QUESTIONS

The multiple-choice section of the eighth grade test includes 45 questions that span the content area of both the seventh and eighth grades. That is what makes this part of the test more difficult than the tests you took during the school year.

If you go back and look at the Intermediate Social Studies State Assessment Specifications Grid, you will notice that there is a range of test questions from every standard and every unit. Therefore, you will find questions dealing with:

- United States and New York history
- world history as it relates to U.S. foreign policy
- geography
- economics
- civics

Knowing this, you must go back and review material you learned in the seventh grade. By doing so, you will have an advantage when it comes time to answer questions related to documents that were part of the seventh grade curriculum.

What type of questions can you expect? Just as in the document-based question section of the test, the multiple-choice section contains questions that deal with historical facts and questions that use maps, graphs, charts, quotes, and cartoons. You will get four answer choices, and later in this chapter you will receive specific clues that should make your task in answering these questions easier.

Here are a few examples of multiple-choice questions previously asked on the New York State standardized tests in social studies.

UNITED STATES HISTORY

In the United States during the late 1800s, increased immigration, the expansion of industry, and improved transportation systems contributed to

1. widespread economic decline.
2. the rapid growth of cities.
3. government ownership of industries.
4. better working conditions in factories.

_____

This question asks you to relate a time period (the late 1800s) with three trends that developed in the United States—increased immigration, the growth of industry, and improvements in transportation. When you put the three trends together, or even if you only know about one of the trends, you should realize that the effect of all three was the rapid growth of cities (2). The other choices are either historically incorrect (1, 3) or not consistent with the time period (4).

NEW YORK STATE HISTORY

Which statement best describes the typical New York farming family in the late 1700s?

1. Family members enjoyed a large amount of leisure time.
2. The family was expected to be nearly self-sufficient.
3. Family members put very little value on the ownership of land.
4. The family depended completely on the government for help in time of need.

_____

There are some very important clues found in the choices that should lead you to the correct response. You can eliminate (1) because of the use of the word *large* in describing the amount of leisure time. (3) characterizes the value of land ownership as "very little" and (4) describes the reliance on the government in time of need as "completely." The correct answer (2) assumes you know the definition of self-sufficient as meaning "not needing others."

WORLD HISTORY AS IT RELATES TO U.S. FOREIGN POLICY

During the 1960s, events in Cuba, East Germany, and Southeast Asia led the United States to believe its interests were threatened by

1. poverty and famine.
2. environmental disaster.
3. the spread of communism.
4. economic depression.

Your ability to relate a common theme, the spread of communism, with events taking place in different parts of the world should lead you to the correct answer (3). The other choices are usually related to domestic concerns.

GEOGRAPHY

The theory that Native American Indians migrated across a land bridge from Asia to settle in North America is based on

1. political studies.
2. archaeological discoveries.
3. diaries written during the migration.
4. modern short stories written by Native American Indians.

If you understand the role of an archaeologist as an investigator who uses relics, you should be able to choose (2) as the correct response. Political studies would give evidence about the role of government and politics in Native American society. Diaries might be used, but they would have to be validated first. And modern short stories would not be valid historical evidence.

ECONOMICS

Throughout United States history, a major goal of tariffs has been to

1. decrease the price of domestic goods.
2. limit competition from foreign goods.
3. improve the quality of imported goods.
4. increase the number of imported goods.

If you know the definition of a tariff (a tax on imported goods), you should have an easy time answering this question. Think of the U.S. government's response when consumers began to choose automobiles made in Japan because they were less expensive than cars made in America. Tariffs were imposed so that the price of Japanese cars would increase and be less competitive with American cars (**2**).

CIVICS

On controversial issues such as prayer in public schools, decisions of the U.S. Supreme Court are based on the Court's interpretation of the

1. Bill of Rights.
2. Articles of Confederation.
3. Declaration of Independence.
4. Emancipation Proclamation.

The Supreme Court's major role is to interpret the Constitution. The Bill of Rights is the only one of the four choices that is part of the U.S. Constitution. The First Amendment in the Bill of Rights deals with the separation of church and state. Therefore (**1**) is the correct response. The other historical documents are all important, but none of them have been interpreted by the Supreme Court.

QUESTIONS THAT USE AN ILLUSTRATION AS A CLUE

Village of North Ocean

BEACH RULES

NO

BICYCLE RIDING
DOGS ALLOWED ON THE BEACH
SOLICITING OR PEDDLING
FOOD OR DRINK ON THE BEACH
ALCOHOLIC BEVERAGES
SWIMMING

ORDINANCES STRICTLY ENFORCED
HAVE A NICE DAY

The beach rules listed in the sign were most probably made by the

1. United States Congress.
2. New York State legislature.
3. New York State governor.
4. North Ocean Village government.

When you look at the sign, you should see immediately that the Village of North Ocean posted the rules (**4**). Therefore, the rules had to be made by the village. You should also reach that conclusion by knowing that Congress makes laws for the entire country; the New York State legislature makes laws for the entire state; and the governor of New York signs laws, but does not make them.

QUESTIONS THAT USE A QUOTATION AS A CLUE

> *Give me your tired, your poor,*
> *Your huddled masses yearning to breathe free, . . .*
> *Send these, the homeless,*
> *tempest-tossed to me:*
> *I lift my lamp beside the golden door.*
>
> —Emma Lazarus, Inscription on the
> Statue of Liberty

This quotation supports a policy of

1. open immigration.
2. expansionism.
3. Manifest Destiny.
4. nativism.

The quote and the inscription are major clues in determining that (**1**) is the correct answer. And if you knew that *nativism* means being opposed to immigration, and that expansionism and Manifest Destiny deal with the movement of U.S. borders to the West Coast, you could eliminate those choices.

QUESTIONS THAT USE A CARTOON AS A CLUE

This cartoon most directly concerns President Theodore Roosevelt's policies concerning

1. the environment.
2. Latin America.
3. social reform.
4. big business.

Theodore Roosevelt established a foreign policy towards Latin America saying the United States should "speak softly, but carry a big stick." The cartoon depicts that policy. It also shows Roosevelt on a boat going to Panama. That's another great clue that should help you recognize the correct response (**2**).

QUESTIONS THAT USE A CHART AS A CLUE

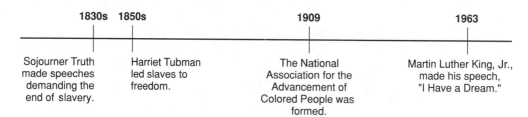

1830s	1850s	1909	1963
Sojourner Truth made speeches demanding the end of slavery.	Harriet Tubman led slaves to freedom.	The National Association for the Advancement of Colored People was formed.	Martin Luther King, Jr., made his speech, "I Have a Dream."

Which statement is supported by the information in the timeline?

1. African-Americans have struggled to gain equal rights throughout U.S. history.
2. Women have made greater contributions to the civil rights movement than men.
3. The civil rights movement ended in 1963.
4. Most efforts to gain rights for African-Americans were started by the federal government.

The timeline reflects attempts by individuals (Sojourner Truth, Harriet Tubman, and Martin Luther King, Jr.) and a private group (The National Association for the Advancement of Colored People) to increase civil rights for African-Americans. That should give you a clue to choose (1) as the correct response. (2) is an opinion. (3) is incorrect, even though the timeline ends in 1963. (4) is wrong because the government is not mentioned in the timeline at all.

So you can see that the multiple-choice section gives you many different questions, all containing clues that can help you choose the right answer.

OVERVIEW OF PART II: CONSTRUCTED RESPONSE QUESTIONS

These document-based questions are more like short answer questions.

- They are keyed to the learning standards found in the scope and sequence.
- They are based on the information found in the document.

- They are factual.
- They may be open-ended, which means you may have to draw conclusions.
- They use different types of documents such as maps, graphs, timelines, cartoons, primary sources, charts, and short readings.
- They usually have three to four questions that "scaffold" or build from simple to complex.
- They are scored using a rubric, a scoring scale, to determine the number of points awarded for each answer.

Part II is worth approximately 20 percent of your total score. The advantages you have in answering these questions over the multiple-choice questions are that you can receive partial credit and the information you need to answer the questions is contained in the documents.

Here is an example of a constructed response question.

Base your answers to questions 1–4 on the poster below:

1. Who ordered the poster to be put up and why?

_____

2. What were the people named in the poster doing?

_____

3. What was happening at the time?

_____

4. What would be the penalty if the people named in the poster were caught?

_____

Question Analysis

For you to receive full credit, you must be able to answer all four questions correctly. Look at the poster for hints. You should recognize the names of Samuel Adams, Patrick Henry, George Washington, Thomas Jefferson, and Thomas Paine. The fact that the poster was put up by order of King George III in July 1776, as stated in the poster itself, is a huge hint. So the answer to the first question is: King George put up the poster.

The "why" part is a bit more difficult because you must understand the words _disloyal_ and _seditious_ as well as _advocating the overthrow of said government_. If you know that _disloyal_ means traitorous and _seditious_ means rebellious, you are on the right track to answering the rest of the question.

Once you know the "why" part, it is easy to understand what the people named in the poster were doing—they were leading a revolution against the king of England. That leads you to the third question, and the date, July 1776, guides you to the correct answer—the onset of the American Revolution.

Here is another example, a headline from the _Charleston Mercury_ newspaper.

THE UNION IS DISSOLVED!
SOUTH CAROLINA SECEDES FROM THE UNITED STATES

Base your answer to questions 1–3 on the newspaper headline and the accompanying story, and your knowledge of social studies.

1. What major event happened on the day this newspaper was published?

_____

2. What document was South Carolina repealing by its actions?

_____

3. What impact did this have on the United States?

_____

Question Analysis

In order to get full credit, you must answer all three questions correctly. The headline clearly states, "The Union is Dissolved!" After you read the account, it becomes clear that the South Carolina legislature voted to secede, or leave the Union. They did this by repealing or refusing to recognize the Constitution of the United States, originally approved by South Carolina in 1788. As a result of this action, other Southern states left the Union and the Civil War began.

The last example is two written accounts of the same event.

Account of the Boston Massacre in the *Boston Gazette*, March 12, 1770:

Four youths were passing the narrow alley leading to Murray's barrack in which a soldier was waving a broadsword. One of the youths asked another to take care of the sword. The soldier resisted and struck the boy on the arm. The boy then struck the soldier with a short stick, and another knocked the soldier down. In less than a minute, ten or twelve soldiers came with drawn sword. Thirty or forty persons, mostly lads, gathered. The soldiers pushed the people to drive them off. Then some lads threw snowballs at the soldiers. At this point, Captain Preston commanded the soldiers to fire.

Account of the Boston Massacre on the engraving on Paul Revere's statue:

Unhappy Boston! See thy sons deplore (view as terrible)
Thy hallowed (sacred) walks besmeared with guiltless gore (blood)
While Faithless Preston and his savage bands
With murderous rancor (anger) stretch their bloody hands
Like fierce barbarians grinning o'er their prey
Approve the carnage (slaughter) and enjoy the day.

1. What event is each of these accounts describing?

2. Which account is more factual?

3. According to the *Boston Gazette*, who started the conflict?

4. According to the engraving on the statue, how did the British react?

Question Analysis

To receive full credit, you must answer all four questions. The first thing you should do is notice that one account of the Boston Massacre is from a newspaper and the other account is from an engraving on a statue of Paul Revere. Immediately you should realize that the newspaper account is more factual, while the engraving's account is more opinionated. Both accounts describe the Boston Massacre, as you can see from their titles. The *Boston Gazette* article described how, after a soldier struck a boy on the arm, a group of boys retaliated and more soldiers came with drawn swords. The crowd reacted and snowballs were thrown. The newspaper then states that Captain Preston ordered his men to fire. Therefore, the newspaper places some blame on the crowd, but the direct blame is placed on Captain Preston for ordering his men to fire. The engraving on Paul Revere's statue is much more emotional in the way it describes the massacre. Using such words as *guiltless gore*, and *murderous rancor*, the engraving places the blame squarely on the British and accuses them of acting like fierce barbarians.

Using a rubric scale of zero to two points, your score would be determined as follows:

- ◼ Two points if you completely and correctly answered each of the four questions.
- ◼ One point if you partially answered the four questions.
- ◼ Zero points if you made no attempt to answer any of the questions or if your responses were wrong.

For a more in-depth treatment of the constructed response section look at the constructed response hints later in this chapter.

OVERVIEW OF PART III: DOCUMENT-BASED QUESTIONS

Part III is a combination of the short answer constructed response document questions *and* an essay based on the scaffolding (building) of each of the six to seven documents presented. Each document-based question, also known as a *DBQ*, will give you specific information including:

- ◼ The theme of the essay
- ◼ The historical context
- ◼ Your task

Your ability to understand the nature of the DBQ will help you organize your essay and better enable you to answer the short answer scaffolding questions. The document-based questions:

- ◼ are based on the Social Studies Scope and Sequence standards.
- ◼ provide you with common documents and common tasks.
- ◼ emphasize critical thinking.

- require you to answer simple factual questions.
- require you to compare and contrast information.
- require you to draw inferences and conclusions.
- require you to analyze different types of documents including maps, graphs, charts, photos, political cartoons, short readings, and primary sources.
- ask you to put together the information you analyzed and write an essay.
- are scored based on a standard rubric.

Here is an example of a Part III document-based question section.

Theme: The Institution of Slavery in Pre-Civil War United States
This task is based on the accompanying documents (1–6). Some of these documents have been edited for the purpose of this task. This task is designed to test your ability to work with historical documents. As you analyze the documents, take into account both the source of each document and the author's point of view.

Historical Context
Throughout history, basic civil and human rights have been denied people through the actions of individuals, groups, and governments. From earliest colonial times until 1865, slavery existed in the United States. What was the purpose of slavery from earliest colonial times until 1865?

Task
Discuss the purpose of slavery from colonial times to the Civil War and how slavery denied people their basic civil and human rights.

Part A—Short Answer
The documents below relate information about slavery in the United States before the Civil War. Examine each document carefully, and then answer the question that follows it. These answers will help you in your Part B essay.

Document 1: Description of a Whipping

My master used to . . . whip me. He would put my hands together and tie them. Then he would strip me naked—He would whip me on one side till that was sore and full of blood and then he would whip me on the other side till that was all tore up.

1. What does this document say about the relationship between slave and master?

_____

_____

Document 2: Slaves Preparing Cotton for the Cotton Gin on a Plantation

© CORBIS

1. Describe the main task performed by the slaves.

_____

_____

2. What is the job of an overseer?

_____

_____

Document 3: Description of a Slave Home

We lodged in log huts and on the bare ground. Wooden floors were an unknown luxury—Our beds were collections of straw and old rags, thrown down in the corners and boxed in with boards, a single blanket the only covering—The wind whistled and the rain and snow blew in through the cracks, and the damp earth soaked in the moisture till the floor was miry as a pigsty. Such were our houses.

1. Identify two specific examples from the document that illustrate the poor living conditions endured by slaves.

_____

_____

Document 4: Description of a Slave Auction

© CORBIS

I was about twelve or fourteen years old when I was sold—I was a boy then big enough to work. I had a brother named John and a cousin by the name of Brutus. Both of them were sold and about three weeks later, it came my turn. On the day I left home, everything was sad among the slaves. My mother and father sung and prayed over me and told me how to get along in the world.

1. What power does the boy's parents have over his future? Why?

_____

_____

Document 5: A Speech by Frederick Douglass (1850)

The law gives the master absolute power over the slave. He may work him, flog him, hire him out, sell him . . . In law a slave has no wife, no children, no country, and no home. He can own nothing, acquire nothing, but what must belong to another.

1. What is Frederick Douglass pointing out about the institution of slavery?

_____

_____

Document 6: A Fugitive Slave Law Poster

© CORBIS

1. To whom is the poster addressed?

_____

_____

2. What is the purpose of the poster and what group is probably responsible for publishing it?

_____

_____

Document 7: "There Is No Such Thing as a Rest"—Solomon Northrop, a Freed Black Man Who was Kidnapped in New York and Sold into Slavery for Twelve Years

The hands are required to be in the cotton field as soon as it is light in the morning, and with the exception of ten or fifteen minutes, which is given them at noon to swallow their allowance of cold bacon, they are not permitted to be a moment idle until it is too dark to see, and when the moon is full, they often times labor till the middle of the night. They do not dare to stop even at dinner time, nor return to the quarters, however late it be, until the order to halt is given by the driver.

1. How long is the workday of the slave?

_____

_____

2. What is the role of the driver?

_____

_____

Part B—Essay

Task

Using the documents above, your answers to the questions in Part A, and your knowledge of social studies, write a well-developed essay that includes an introduction, supporting paragraphs, and a conclusion, in which you describe the lives of slaves in the United States before the Civil War. In your essay you should discuss the purposes of slavery from colonial times to the Civil War and how slavery denied people their basic civil and human rights.

Rubric
Document-Based Question

5

- Thoroughly addresses all aspects of the Task by accurately analyzing and interpreting at least four documents
- Incorporates information from the documents in the body of the essay
- Incorporates relevant outside information
- Richly supports the theme or problem with relevant facts, examples, and details
- Is a well-developed essay, consistently demonstrating a logical and clear plan of organization
- Introduces the theme or problem by establishing a framework that is beyond a simple restatement of the Task or Historical Context and concludes with a summation of the theme or problem

4

- Addresses all aspects of the Task by accurately analyzing and interpreting at least four documents
- Incorporates information from the documents in the body of the essay
- Incorporates relevant outside information
- Includes relevant facts, examples, and details, but discussion may be more descriptive than analytical
- Is a well-developed essay, demonstrating a logical and clear plan of organization
- Introduces the theme or problem by establishing a framework that is beyond a simple restatement of the Task or Historical Context and concludes with a summation of the theme or problem

3

- Addresses most aspects of the Task or addresses all aspects of the Task in a limited way, using some of the documents
- Incorporates some information from the documents in the body of the essay
- Incorporates limited or no relevant outside information
- Includes some facts, examples, and details, but discussion is more descriptive than analytical

- ■ Is a satisfactorily developed essay, demonstrating a general plan of organization
- ■ Introduces the theme or problem by repeating the Task or Historical Context and concludes by simply repeating the theme or problem

2

- ■ Attempts to address some aspects of the Task, making limited use of the documents
- ■ Presents no relevant outside information
- ■ Includes few facts, examples, and details; discussion restates contents of the documents
- ■ Is a poorly organized essay, lacking focus
- ■ Fails to introduce or summarize the theme or problem

1

- ■ Shows limited understanding of the Task with vague, unclear references to the documents
- ■ Presents no relevant outside information
- ■ Includes little or no accurate or relevant facts, details, or examples
- ■ Attempts to complete the Task, but demonstrates a major weakness in organization
- ■ Fails to introduce or summarize the theme or problem

0

- ■ Fails to address the Task, is illegible, or is a blank paper

PART A: ANSWERING THE DOCUMENT-BASED QUESTIONS

Let's look at the way you should answer the short answer document-based questions. First, read closely the introductory information provided. Right away you know the documents all deal with pre-Civil War slavery. After you read the historical introduction and the task, it should be even clearer that the documents will lead you to a path that focuses on the institution of slavery and how it impacted the history of the United States.

Once you understand the common thread among the documents, you should answer each question the same way you answered the constructed response questions. Look at the information, and relate it to the questions that are asked. In most cases, you should be able to pick out the answer directly from the document itself.

Scoring Rubric for the Scaffolding Documents

- Two points for a complete answer with examples
- One point for a partial answer
- Zero points for no attempt or a wrong answer

Document 1: Description of a Whipping

The question asks you to find a relationship between the slave and the master. The first sentence couldn't be any clearer—the master whips the slave. The document then describes the whipping in detail. To get full credit, you must describe the hostile relationship between the slave and the master. You should give at least one example from the passage.

Document 2: Slaves Preparing Cotton for the Cotton Gin on a Plantation

The two questions are related to each other. The first question asks about the role of the slave. The second question asks you to determine what the job of an overseer is. You must know the definition of *overseer* to answer the second question. The illustration depicts slaves working on the cotton that was picked in the fields. A person is standing watching over the slaves. He is the overseer. If you talk about the slaves working in the fields, picking cotton, and getting it ready for export (the title of the illustration gives you a big hint), you will get full credit. Knowing that an overseer is a person who watches over what the slaves are doing will get you full credit for the second question.

Document 3: Description of a Slave Home

The question is asking you to find two examples of the poor living conditions slaves endured. So you should look at the passage and pick out words that illustrate some of these terrible living conditions—beds made of straw and old rags, a single blanket even in winter, sleeping on a bare ground. You will get full credit for picking two examples; partial credit for one example; and no credit for a wrong answer or if you made no attempt to answer the question.

Document 4: Description of a Slave Auction

This document gives you two pieces of information—a picture of a slave being auctioned and a description, from a slave's perspective, of what it is like being sold on the auction block. The question asks you to reach a conclusion about the ability of the slave's parents to affect the slave's future. Though the passage does not directly answer that question, it does indicate that the mother and father sing and pray and are optimistic about what is going to happen to the slave. Therefore, while the parents did not have any direct power, they are hopeful that the slave will be able to make a future for himself by listening to their advice. The "why" part of the question flows from that answer. The parents do not have any direct power over the slave because the slave is being sold at auction. To get full credit, you must answer both parts of the question.

Document 5: A Speech by Frederick Douglass (1850)

This is probably the most difficult of the six documents. This speech was made by a former slave who became one of the leading Abolitionists (a person who believed that slavery should be abolished). The question wants you to summarize Douglass' point of view about slavery. If you recognized who Douglass was before reading the passage, you would be looking for key words that indicate his hatred of slavery. Douglass' hatred can be seen in the words he uses in the speech, like a master's "absolute power" over a slave. Douglass' descriptions of a master's harsh treatment of a slave and of a slave's lack of basic rights also indicate his hatred of slavery. To get full credit, you must give a solid example of what Douglass is saying about slavery and how much he hates it.

Document 6: A Fugitive Slave Law Poster

The document describes what happens to a slave who tries to escape from his master under the Fugitive Slave Law, which was passed by Congress and signed by President Buchanan. The law made it illegal for slaves to run away from their masters and offered a reward to anybody who caught an escaped slave. Knowing this background information makes it easier to answer the two questions. The poster is aimed at white people, to encourage them to turn in runaway slaves. The purpose of the poster is to advertise the fact that a reward would be given for the return of an escaped slave to his master. Knowing this, it should be obvious that slave owners would be responsible for putting up these posters. To get full credit, you must completely answer the first question and both parts of the second question.

Document 7: "There Is No Such Thing as Rest"

This last document describes the typical workday of the slave. This is an important document to use in addressing the task in the essay portion of the document-based question. It clearly shows that the slave worked from sunrise to well past sunset. It also illustrates the role of the slave driver as being in complete control of the slave's work schedule. To get full credit, your answer must indicate that the slave's workday began at sunrise and lasted past sunset and that the role of the driver was to be in charge of the slave, telling the slave how long the workday was.

PART B: WRITING THE ESSAY

Before writing the essay, develop a boxed outline of the essay. This outline includes the key components of your written essay, a rephrasing of the task, your introduction, four examples of documents supporting your answer to the task question, outside information, and a conclusion.

Task	Introduction	Document Support of Task	Document Support of Task	Document Support of Task	Document Support of Task	Outside Information	Conclusion
A. Purpose of slavery. **B.** How slavery denied people of their civil rights.	From Colonial times to the Civil War, Southerners maintained the institution of slavery. It was called the "Peculiar Institution." As a result, slaves were treated harshly and denied their civil rights.	*Number 1 supports Task B* Harsh treatment by masters; helped maintain discipline and denied civil rights.	*Number 2 supports Task A* Slaves working on a plantation illustrates the main purpose of slavery. It also shows how the South needed slaves for their economy.	*Number 4 supports Task B* A slave auction is a good example of how slaves were denied their civil rights.	*Number 5 supports Task B* Frederick Douglass describes his life as a former slave. This shows that slaves were treated very harshly.	Cotton gin as a factor in the need for slavery. Fugitive slave laws; *Dred Scott* case.	The South believed that their economy could not survive without slavery. The plantation system and the production of cotton created a need for slaves. Unfortunately, the treatment of slaves had the result of denying them civil rights.

Once you have completed a boxed outline that incorporates your answers to the documents, it should be a relatively easy task to write an essay that describes the lives of slaves in the United States before the Civil War. Notice that the directions tell you step-by-step what you should do. Later in this chapter, you will get specific pointers on how to better organize your essay.

In the general introduction to the essay, you should begin your task by outlining the information you need to answer the question following the format that you are given in the essay's task:

- ■ Introduction: give a sentence or two rephrasing the fact that slaves had a very difficult life before the Civil War.
- ■ Body of the essay: write three to five paragraphs restating the information you find in the documents. You should go back to the documents and pick out the most compelling information on the terrible lives slaves had. This is the heart of the essay. Some of the information you should provide includes the harsh treatment of the slaves by their masters (**Document 1**), the kinds of jobs that a slave performs (**Document 2**), their terrible living conditions (**Documents 3** and **7**), a slave's description of what it felt like being sold (**Document 4**), and what would happen to a slave who tried to escape from his master (**Documents 5** and **6**). You don't have to include information from every document, but you must include relevant facts from most of them to get full credit. In addition to referring back to the documents, you should bring in any historical information you know that relates to the question. For instance, you can include the fact that Eli Whitney's cotton gin made slavery essential to the Southern economy. You could discuss how slaves were brought into the country during colonial times and how the Constitution permitted slave trade until the early 1800s. You should identify Frederick Douglass as a former slave.
- ■ The conclusion: the last paragraph should summarize in one or two sentences the major point that you made in the essay—that slavery before the Civil War was a terrible institution that has left a lasting negative impression that is still felt today.
- ■ Your score on the essay: if you look closely at the generic (general) rubric scale, you should immediately see that in order to get full credit, you must follow the format found in the directions of the essay's task. Therefore, even if you wrote an essay that completely answered the question, but you did not provide an introduction or conclusion, you would not receive full credit.

CLUES, HINTS, AND POINTERS

This part of the chapter is aimed at improving your test-taking skills by looking at the different components of the test—the multiple-choice section, the constructed response section, and the document-based essay. It is divided into multiple-choice clues, constructed response hints, and document-based essay pointers.

MULTIPLE-CHOICE CLUES

The questions for this section have been taken from previous New York State Standardized tests. Remember that Part I of the test is worth 50 percent of your score and that you will have 45 minutes to finish it.

General Clues

> CLUE 1
>
> Read the entire question and all answer choices.

Suggestions:

- Look at the question, and if you are familiar with the topic, come up with a possible answer.
- Use the process of elimination to help you when you are looking at the choices.
- Then look at *all* the choices. Odds are that the answer you had in mind will be one of the four choices.

> CLUE 2
>
> Choose the answer that comes to your mind first.

Suggestions:

- After reading the entire question and the four choices, you may narrow your choices down to two possibilities.
- Go with your first instinct. It is probably going to be the correct answer.

> ### CLUE 3
>
> Think of classroom activities that relate to the topic of the question.

Suggestions:

- Your teacher has worked very hard during the year to prepare you for this test.
- There have been many activities that you completed in class and for homework. They include films, group work, discussions, computer activities as well as other activities.
- When you see the question, think back to the different things you did in class. You'll be surprised at how those activities will help you figure out the correct answer.

> ### CLUE 4
>
> Don't be concerned about the pattern of the answers.

Suggestions:

- Many students look at the pattern of answers when they take tests. If they see two answers that have (**1**) as the correct response, they are hesitant to choose the next answer as (**1**).
- Answer each question independently from the last question.

> ### CLUE 5
>
> Be aware that the test questions are generally organized in a chronological order.

Suggestions:

- The multiple-choice section of this test usually follows the chronological order of the units you studied.
- If you are aware of this, you can anticipate the order of the questions and concentrate on one specific unit at a time.

Specific Clues

CLUE 6

Underline key words.

As you take the test, you should get in the habit of answering each of the questions the same way. This includes underlining key words and key phrases in the question. Most of the time the correct answer will relate to one of the underlined phrases.

Example: Which area of the world was affected by the <u>Monroe Doctrine</u>, the <u>"Big Stick" policy</u>, and the <u>Good Neighbor Policy</u>?

1. Eastern Europe
2. Latin America
3. Africa
4. Southeast Asia

By underlining each of the key words (even if you are only able to identify one of them), you should notice that each underlined phrase relates to Latin America (**2**).

CLUE 7

Cross out wrong choices.

Once you have underlined the key words or phrases in the question, you should cross out answers you know to be incorrect.

Example: In U.S. history, the years between <u>1865 and 1914</u> could best be characterized as a period of

1. slavery and sectionalism.
2. immigration and industrialization.
3. aggression and appeasement.
4. communism and containment.

By crossing out obvious incorrect choices (1), (3), and (4), you are left with the correct answer (2). You can cross out those choices because none of them relate to the time period you underlined.

CLUE 8

Guess if you can eliminate one of the answers.

This clue will probably be one that you will find most helpful. Odds are that you will be able to eliminate at least one incorrect answer in every question. Remember to cross it out. An educated guess is always better than picking out any answer.

Example: Base your answer on the newspaper headlines below and on your knowledge of social studies.

"BLACK TUESDAY: STOCKS HIT ALL-TIME LOW"
"ROOSEVELT PROMISES A NEW DEAL FOR ALL AMERICANS"
"UNEMPLOYMENT HITS A NEW HIGH: 20% AND CLIMBING!"

These headlines reflect which period in U.S. history?

1. The Progressive Era
2. The Roaring Twenties
3. The Great Depression
4. World War II

Because the headlines all deal with one time period, you can certainly eliminate at least one of the choices. Because there is no mention of a war, (4) is the best one to eliminate first. The headlines all have one common characteristic—they are all about economics and a period of economic decline. The hints you get from the headlines include the stock market crash, Franklin Roosevelt is the president, and a high unemployment rate. The answer then is the Great Depression (3).

> ### CLUE 9
>
> If you guess, look for something familiar.

Always have your detective tools handy and look at the question closely. This is especially true when the question is a diagram, cartoon, or drawing.

MOVING ASSEMBLY LINE

Example: The process shown in the drawing is

1. job sharing.
2. a system of mass production.
3. the domestic system.
4. the Bessemer method.

If you look at the drawing, the fact that men are building automobiles should jump out at you. Then you should notice the words "interchangeable parts" and "moving assembly line." Put these familiar things together and you should realize that the drawing relates to a system of mass production (2).

> ### CLUE 10
>
> Use logic.

One of the best ways to attack these questions is through pure logic. If the answer seems correct, it probably is right.

Example: Which is a primary source of evidence that Columbus sailed to find a new route to the Indies in 1492?

1. A television show about the explorations of Columbus.
2. A letter from the current ambassador from Spain describing the voyage.
3. A painting showing Columbus landing in the New World.
4. A diary entry written by a crewmember aboard Columbus' ship.

Using logic, and even if you do not know what a primary source is, you should realize that the first three choices are all accounts made in the present and that a diary entry comes from the time period of the event. Therefore, you would know that (4) is the correct answer.

> ### CLUE 11
>
> Be a detective and look for clues.

The title of this section is "Multiple-Choice Clues." A good detective solves problems by finding and using clues. Every question has a clue. Find it and you will be able to correctly answer the question.

Example: What do the hats in the cartoon represent?

1. The political offices a person must hold before becoming president.
2. The different positions a president must fill with qualified people.
3. The different roles a president has while in office.
4. The official titles the president holds after leaving office.

The clues in this question are the button the person is wearing ("president") and the different hats on the man's head, representing the different duties that the president performs. When you put these clues together, you should come up with right answer (3).

CLUE 12

Eliminate answers that have absolutes. Words like *all*, *every*, and *none* are examples of absolutes.

This is probably the easiest clue to apply to a multiple-choice question. Words like *all*, *every*, *none*, *best*, and *worst* usually signal a wrong answer.

Example: Today in cities such as New York, Hong Kong, Cairo, and Mexico City, many people wear blue jeans and drink colas made in the United States. They use French perfume and buy Japanese cameras. The best explanation for this situation is that

1. all these places are alike because they are controlled by the United States.
2. most places in the world have the same culture.
3. U.S. products are used worldwide because they are the best.
4. increased communication and trade have decreased the cultural differences between parts of the world.

Since choices (1) and (3) contain absolutes, you can immediately eliminate them. Common sense should tell you that (2) is incorrect. And there are certainly enough hints in the question itself to suggest that there are fewer cultural differences between parts of the world (4).

CLUE 13

Look for general statements that make sense.

More often than not, the correct answer is phrased in a way that makes the most sense out of the choices offered. So remember to compare the choice you feel is the most sensible to the others before making your final selection.

Example: About 60,000 native *Tainos* were living on the island now called Puerto Rico when Columbus' expedition first arrived. In less than 20 years, the native *Taino* population was about 2,000. Which statement best explains the decrease in the native population?

1. The Spanish moved most of the natives to other locations.
2. Most of the natives intermarried with the Spanish.
3. The natives could not adjust to the new Spanish religion.
4. The natives were exposed to diseases brought by the Europeans.

Logic dictates that Spain would not move 60,000 people to other locations. There is also no reason why intermarriage with the Spanish, or a new religion would have decreased the native population so drastically. Sickness and death caused by disease certainly would explain the decrease in population. Thus, the only answer that makes sense is (4).

> CLUE 14
>
> Don't fall for traps.

Many questions give you clues regarding time periods. They may ask you about a specific time period, or they may talk about a specific event, or they may make reference to a particular person. If you can connect the question to a particular event or period, you can easily eliminate choices that don't relate to the question and try to trap you.

Example: In the late 1800s, some Americans believed that a powerful country had the right to control territory outside its borders. Which term refers to this belief?

1. Communism
2. Imperialism
3. Isolationism
4. Totalitarianism

Once you identify the time period as the late 1800s, you can eliminate the trap answers. (1), (3), and (4) are obviously wrong because they do not relate to that era. The only choice that is correct is (2), which fits within the definition of imperialism as the right of a country to control territory outside its borders.

CLUE 15

Look for obvious incorrect statements.

Any question that asks you for an obvious answer will usually have obvious incorrect statements as answer choices.

Example: Which function is carried out by both the federal and state governments?

1. collecting taxes
2. declaring war
3. appointing ambassadors
4. coining money

You are looking for things that both the federal and state governments do, so it stands to reason that the only function that both perform is collecting taxes (1). Only the federal government (Congress) can declare war, appoint ambassadors (the president), and coin money (Congress).

CLUE 16

Look for obvious correct choices.

The reverse of Clue 15 is also true. If what a question is asking you is obvious, you will probably find that the correct choice is also obvious.

Example: The legislature of New York State consists of the

1. Court of Appeals and the State Supreme Court.
2. House of Representatives and the Senate.
3. Governor and the Lieutenant Governor.
4. Senate and the Assembly.

You should know that a legislature consists of two law-making bodies, and therefore, you can narrow your choices down to (2) and (4). Since the House of Representatives is paired with the Senate in (2), and they are both associated with the federal government, you can eliminate (2) as the correct choice. That leaves the obvious choice of the Senate and Assembly (4). This question becomes even easier if you put the word *state* in front of Senate (State Senate) and Assembly (State Assembly). They have a familiar ring, don't they?

> CLUE 17
>
> Find any obvious differences among the answers given.

Once you recognize what the question is asking, you should be able to detect any major differences between the choices offered. The choice that best relates to any hint given is usually going to be the correct response.

Example: "The American continents . . . are . . . not to be considered as subjects for future colonization by any European powers . . ."
This passage is taken from the

1. Mayflower Compact
2. Monroe Doctrine
3. Gettysburg Address
4. Fourteen Points

Looking at the quote, you should be able to figure out that America was no longer a colony at the time the statement was made, and eliminate (1). You should also be able to determine that the passage was directed at European powers, and eliminate (3). Since (4) relates to President Wilson's plans for a proposed peace treaty, and not a warning to Europe, you are left with the Monroe Doctrine (2). By recognizing the differences between the choices offered, you have eliminated all incorrect answers.

CLUE 18

Be careful not to choose an answer that, while accurate, has nothing to do with the question.

Example: The trials of Dred Scott, Homer Plessy, and Ernesto Miranda demonstrate the role of the courts in determining the

1. use of the death penalty.
2. rights of the individual.
3. right of privacy.
4. length of prison sentences.

Even though courts have dealt with issues like the death penalty, the right of privacy, and length of prison sentences, the trials of Dred Scott, Homer Plessy, and Ernesto Miranda all had to do with the rights of each of those individuals. Scott was fighting for his freedom from slavery; Plessy was arguing for equal protection under the law; and Miranda was accusing the police of denying him his basic due process rights.

Thus, while the statements contained in (1), (3), and (4) are accurate, they do not relate to the question and are incorrect choices.

CONSTRUCTED RESPONSE HINTS

The hints contained in this section are based on documents researched by the staff of the Northport-East Northport School District, as well as documents prepared by the New York State Education Department. Remember, this part of the test is worth 20 percent of your score and you will have 45 minutes to complete it.

General Hints

HINT 1

Identify the type of document involved.

The documents in the constructed response section of the test vary in form. The documents can be cartoons, drawings, reading passages, graphs, charts, timelines, or any other related material. The New York State Social Studies Scope and Sequence has a recommended list of documents. This list can be found on page 136.

HINT 2

Be aware of the time period that is being tested.

These documents ask you to answer questions about a definite time period. Once you have identified the nature of the document and found the hints contained within, answer the questions using evidence from the documents and your knowledge of history. Do not use the same words found in the documents. Summarize the data and use your own words.

HINT 3

Go over the rubric before answering the questions.

Remember, the constructed response section is worth 20 percent of the test and each question has a zero to two scoring scale. This scale awards credit as follows:

- Two points if you completely and correctly answered each of the four questions.
- One point if you partially answered the four questions.
- Zero points if you made no attempt to answer any of the questions or if your responses were wrong.

HINT 4

As you look at the document and find the hints, take notes in the margin of the test book.

As you investigate the document and find the hints, write them down in the margin of the test book before you start answering the questions.

HINT 5

If the document is a reading passage, look for a point of view. Also look for vocabulary words that may give you an idea as to the general theme of the question.

Example: Statement by President Franklin Roosevelt after signing the Social Security Act in 1935:

The social security measure gives at least some protection to 30 million of our citizens who will reap direct benefits through unemployment compensation, and through increased services for the protection of ill health. We can never insure 100 percent of the population against 100 percent of the hazards and vicissitudes (uncertainties) of life, but we have tried to frame a law which will give some measure of protection to the average citizen and to his family against the loss of a job and against poverty-ridden (stricken) old age.

1. What is the purpose of the statement?

_____

_____

2. What is the major goal of the Social Security Act?

_____

_____

3. How does the Social Security Act illustrate Roosevelt's belief in the role of the federal government?

_____

_____

Look at the title of the passage; it is a hint as to the purpose of the statement—an explanation of the law's purpose. In addition, the fact that Roosevelt signed the act in 1935 identifies the law as part of the New Deal. As you read the passage, you see immediately that the primary goal of Social Security was to protect 30 million people by giving them an income after they retire. The second paragraph points out the role of the federal government in passing this law. Roosevelt states that he believes it is the role of government to help people avoid poverty as they grow older.

HINT 6

If the document is a cartoon, look for the point the cartoonist is trying to make.

The cartoonist may be poking fun at a politician or illustrating problems that the country is facing. Some cartoons are very sarcastic. Others may be very complimentary. When you look at a cartoon, look for the hints. They may be found in the caption or in the labels on things pictured within the cartoon. Sometimes they are found in the symbols the cartoonist uses.

Example: "Lincoln's Dilemma"

CAN HE FILL'EM?

1. What point is the cartoonist trying to make about Lincoln?

_____

_____

2. What do the lions symbolize?

_____

_____

3. Why is Lincoln holding a chair and a whip?

_____

_____

4. What constitutional crisis is Lincoln trying to deal with?

_____

_____

In determining the cartoonist's point, you should notice the location of the cartoon's caption. The caption is found by his shoes and the caption asks, "Can he fill 'em?" This is a very important hint. The cartoon illustrates that Lincoln is faced with the threat of the South's secession from the Union, and questions as to whether he could succeed in resolving the crisis. The caption represents the old saying that a leader must be able to fill the shoes he or she is wearing and the shoes represent Lincoln's ability to resolve sectional differences. The lions represent the sectional dispute between North and South. Lincoln is trying to "tame" them by bringing both the North and South together before a civil war breaks out.

HINT 7

If the document is a graph, identify the information contained within it.

Graphs provide information. So, the first thing you must do is to identify the information contained in the graph. You should look for the title of the graph. Then look for labels and, finally, try to understand what they all mean. If you use these hints, you are well on your way to answering the questions.

Example: Production of Corn vs. Prices of Corn

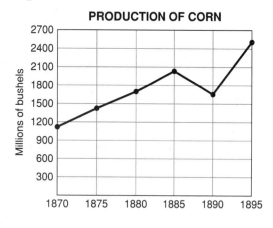
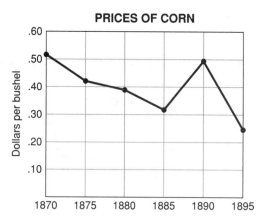

1. In what year was the largest quantity of corn produced?

_____

_____

2. What was the trend in corn prices between 1870 and 1885?

_____

_____

3. Describe the effect of decreasing corn production on the price of corn.

_____

_____

4. Identify the economic principle that accounts for the relationship between the amount of corn production and the price.

_____

_____

The titles of the graphs are "Production of Corn" and "Price of Corn." The labels on the graph for the "Production of Corn" are the amount of bushels produced from 1870–1895. The labels on the "Price of Corn" are the dollars per bushel from 1870–1895. You should easily identify the largest quantity of corn produced by looking at the peak of the graph (2,400 bushels). Looking at the corn prices between 1870 and 1885, it is obvious the price per bushel went down from approximately 50 cents a bushel to 30 cents a bushel. Looking at that trend, you should conclude that as the production of corn increases, the price of corn decreases. This is called the law of supply and demand.

> HINT 8
>
> If the document is a chart, identify the information provided within it.

Like the graph, the first thing you should do is look for the name of the chart. Then look at the information that the chart conveys. Once you have done that, you should be able to answer the questions.

Example: "Labor Union Membership 1900–1945"

LABOR UNIONS

Year	AFL	CIO	Independent Unions	Total Membership
1900	548		243	791
1905	1,494		424	1,918
1910	1,562		554	2,116
1915	1,946		614	2,560
1920	4,079		955	5,034
1925	2,877		689	3,566
1930	2,961		671	3,632
1935	3,218		535	3,753
1940	4,343	2,154	785	7,682
1945	6,890	3,928	1,744	12,562

LABOR UNION MEMBERSHIP* 1900–1945

SOURCE: *U.S. Census Bureau*   * in thousands

1. What is the subject of this chart?

_____

_____

2. What was the total of labor union membership in 1910?

_____

_____

3. Why was there a change in total labor union membership between 1900–1945?

_____

_____

4. What other trend can you identify from this table?

_____

_____

The title of the chart is "Labor Union Membership 1900–1945." The information contained in the chart includes individual labor union membership for specific years and overall union membership for the same years. The total membership of labor unions in 1910 was 2,116,000 (remember the figures represented are all in thousands, so you have to multiply each number by 1000). Total labor union membership increased between 1900 and 1945 because more unions were formed as the country became more industrialized. Labor unions also grew as they became more successful in getting benefits for their members. Another trend you can identify is the formation of a new labor union in 1940, the CIO. This union eventually joined with the AFL and became the second largest union in the country.

HINT 9

If there is a time component contained within a document, identify the time period and any events related to the information provided.

Think about the historical time period the document relates to and draw upon any information you know about that particular time.

Example: "United States Fatalities in Major Wars"

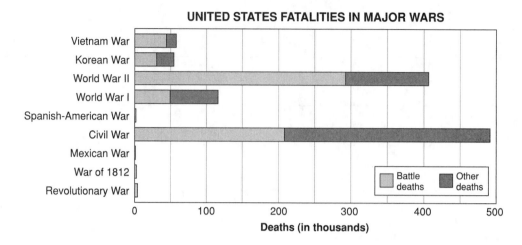

1. Identify the decades during which the Spanish-American War, World War I, and the Korean War took place. Which of those wars had the most fatalities?

_____

_____

2. In which war did the fewest number of Americans die?

_____

_____

3. In which war did the most Americans die in battle?

_____

_____

4. List two factors that explain why deaths may increase or decrease from war to war.

_____

_____

The title of this time period graph is "United States Fatalities in Major Wars." One side lists the names of the wars the United States has been involved in. The other side lists U.S. deaths in thousands. Based upon your knowledge of history, you should be able to identify the decade that each of the wars took place—the Spanish-American War in the 1890s, World War I in the 1910s, and the Korean War in the 1950s. The Mexican War had the fewest casualties; the Civil War had the most. Factors that influence the number of casualties include the length of the war, the weapons available, and where the war was fought.

> HINT 10
>
> Look for key phrases or words in the document itself.

Many times a reading passage taken from an eyewitness account will have emotional words. Look to them as a way of determining the point of view of the passage.

Example:

At first, the frontier was the Atlantic coast. It was the frontier of Europe in a very real sense. Moving westward, the frontier became more and more American. As successive terminal moraines result from successive glaciations, so each frontier leaves its traces behind it, and when it becomes a settled area the region still partakes of the frontier characteristics. Thus the advance of the frontier has meant a steady movement away from the influence of Europe, a steady growth of independence on American lines. And to study this advance, the men who grew up under these conditions, and the political, economic, and social results of it, is to study the really American part of our history . . .

Frederick Jackson Turner, _The Frontier in American History._

1. What point is Turner making about the American frontier?

_____

_____

2. What does Turner claim to be the "really American part of our history"?

_____

_____

3. What is the relationship between Manifest Destiny and Turner's point of view?

_____

_____

4. In the expansion of the American frontier what group suffered the most?

_____

_____

Though this is a very difficult passage, you can see that it deals with the movement of pioneers westward. Turner's point of view is made clear when he states that the movement westward reduces the influence of Europe and creates an independent American society. He is so enthusiastic about the western expansion that he claims, "to study this advance . . . is to study the really American part of our history . . ." Manifest Destiny, the belief that it was God's will for America to expand its borders from coast to coast, fits closely with Turner's point of view. And, of course, Native Americans suffered the most as a result of the settlement of America's western frontier.

HINT 11

Study the different parts of a map and look for geographical and historical information contained within.

Maps provide a wealth of information. From geographical patterns to the history of an era, you should be able to find enough valuable information to answer a question correctly.

Example: "The First U.S. Congress 1789–1791"

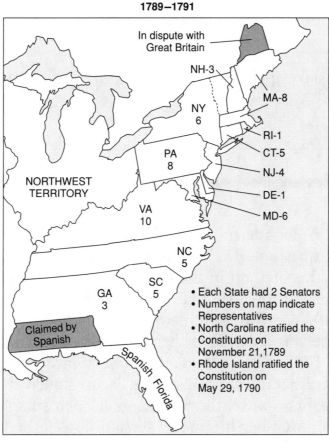

THE FIRST U.S. CONGRESS
1789–1791

In dispute with Great Britain

NH-3

NY 6

MA-8

RI-1

CT-5

PA 8

NJ-4

NORTHWEST TERRITORY

DE-1

MD-6

VA 10

NC 5

SC 5

GA 3

Claimed by Spanish

Spanish Florida

• Each State had 2 Senators
• Numbers on map indicate Representatives
• North Carolina ratified the Constitution on November 21,1789
• Rhode Island ratified the Constitution on May 29, 1790

1. What do the different numbers in each state represent?

---

2. Based on the map, which state had the largest representation in Congress?

_____

_____

3. How did the representation in Congress reflect a compromise reached at the Constitutional Convention?

_____

_____

4. What part did slaves play in the number of representatives Southern states had?

_____

_____

The map is full of wonderful information. The title itself gives you the answer to the first question. The numbers on the map represent the number of congressmen each state had in the first Congress. Once you answer the first question, you should realize that Virginia had the largest number of representatives (10). You should remember from your classroom studies that a great compromise was reached at the Constitutional Convention that met in Philadelphia in 1789. The agreement, between large states and small states, created a bicameral (two-house) legislature called the Congress. Membership in the first house, the Senate, gave each state equal representation (two senators). Membership in the second house, the House of Representatives, based representation on the number of people living in the state. Therefore, a small state like Rhode Island had two senators and one member in the House of Representatives. New York also had two senators, but because it had a larger population than Rhode Island, it had six members of the House. What about slaves? Another compromise, the Three-Fifths Compromise, was also reached in Philadelphia. That agreement counted every five slaves as three people for purposes of determining representation in the House of Representatives. As a result, Southern states were able to increase the number of representatives they sent to Congress.

HINT 12

Note how the questions go from simple to more complex.

The constructed response section of the test starts off with a general or specific question that allows you to find its answer in the document itself. The second question gets a bit harder by asking you to make a connection between different parts of the same document. For instance, it may ask you to compare two things, make a conclusion, or put things in your own words. The third and fourth question are even more difficult and ask you to draw on your knowledge of social studies and other outside information for the correct answers.

Example: "Hunters Reach the Americas"

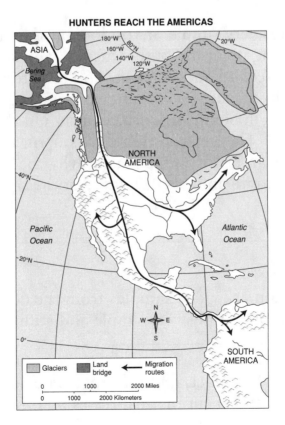

HUNTERS REACH THE AMERICAS

1. What continent did the hunters come from?

_____

_____

2. As the hunters crossed the land bridge in what direction did they travel?

_____

_____

3. Give two reasons why the hunters came to North America.

_____

_____

The first question is very simple. If you look at the hunters' starting point in Asia and their ending point in South America, you should see that they came from Asia. The second question asks you to determine the direction the hunters traveled by tracing their route from Asia. Because their route starts in Asia and ends in South America, you should realize that the hunters traveled south. The last question draws upon your knowledge of an early period in American history. One reason why the hunters came to the Americas was to find more animals to hunt. Another reason was to find a better climate.

HINT 13

If the question asks for examples from the document, make sure you keep your answers simple and straight to the point.

If the question asks for a fact, find a factual statement. If it wants you to find an opinion, find a statement that expresses a point of view.

Example: "An Editorial from the Gannett Newspapers"

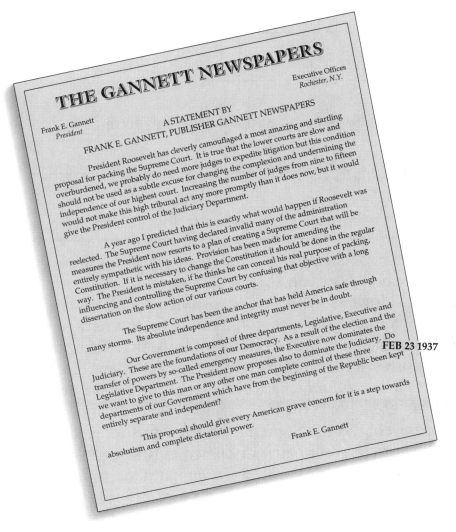

THE GANNETT NEWSPAPERS

Executive Offices
Rochester, N.Y.

Frank E. Gannett
President

A STATEMENT BY
FRANK E. GANNETT, PUBLISHER GANNETT NEWSPAPERS

President Roosevelt has cleverly camouflaged a most amazing and startling proposal for packing the Supreme Court. It is true that the lower courts are slow and overburdened, we probably do need more judges to expedite litigation but this condition should not be used as a subtle excuse for changing the complexion and undermining the independence of our highest court. Increasing the number of judges from nine to fifteen would not make this high tribunal act any more promptly than it does now, but it would give the President control of the Judiciary Department.

A year ago I predicted that this is exactly what would happen if Roosevelt was reelected. The Supreme Court having declared invalid many of the administration measures the President now resorts to a plan of creating a Supreme Court that will be entirely sympathetic with his ideas. Provision has been made for amending the Constitution. If it is necessary to change the Constitution it should be done in the regular way. The President is mistaken, if he thinks he can conceal his real purpose of packing, influencing and controlling the Supreme Court by confusing that objective with a long dissertation on the slow action of our various courts.

The Supreme Court has been the anchor that has held America safe through many storms. Its absolute independence and integrity must never be in doubt.

Our Government is composed of three departments, Legislative, Executive and Judiciary. These are the foundations of our Democracy. As a result of the election and the transfer of powers by so-called emergency measures, the Executive now dominates the Legislative Department. The President now proposes also to dominate the Judiciary. Do we want to give to this man or any other one man complete control of these three departments of our Government which have from the beginning of the Republic been kept entirely separate and independent?

This proposal should give every American grave concern for it is a step towards absolutism and complete dictatorial power.

Frank E. Gannett

FEB 23 1937

1. Identify one fact that is contained in the letter.

---

2. Identify one opinion that is contained in the letter.

---

3. Identify the historical event that the letter is discussing.

_____

_____

4. What point of view is being expressed in this letter?

_____

_____

The title of the document is "A Statement by Frank E. Gannett, Publisher Gannett Newspapers," so you should assume that it contains the opinions of Mr. Gannett. However, you should also find factual statements that back up Gannett's opinions. One fact stated in the fourth paragraph is that the government is made up of three branches: legislative, executive, and judicial. An opinion expressed in the statement is that President Roosevelt's proposal to "pack" the Court _should_ (the word that expresses an opinion) give every American great concern. Once you see that the statement deals with President Roosevelt and the Supreme Court, you should be able to figure out that the historical event being discussed is Roosevelt's attempt to put judges on the Supreme Court who were sympathetic to his causes. Gannett opposes that proposal, which is the main point of view expressed in the statement.

HINT 14

If you find parts of the document too difficult to understand, pick out phrases that you do understand to get information about its point of view and historical setting.

The key to success in the constructed response section is your ability to grasp the main idea expressed by the document presented. Once you do that, you are on your way to successfully answering the questions.

Example: "Japanese Evacuation Order"

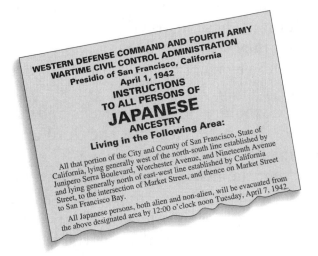

WESTERN DEFENSE COMMAND AND FOURTH ARMY
WARTIME CIVIL CONTROL ADMINISTRATION
Presidio of San Francisco, California
April 1, 1942
INSTRUCTIONS
TO ALL PERSONS OF
JAPANESE
ANCESTRY
Living in the Following Area:

All that portion of the City and County of San Francisco, State of California, lying generally west of the north-south line established by Junipero Serra Boulevard, Worchester Avenue, and Nineteenth Avenue and lying generally north of east-west line established by California Street, to the intersection of Market Street, and thence on Market Street to San Francisco Bay.

All Japanese persons, both alien and non-alien, will be evacuated from the above designated area by 12:00 o'clock noon Tuesday, April 7, 1942.

1. Who is ordering the evacuation of Japanese people in America?

_____

_____

2. What do "alien" and "non-alien" persons mean?

_____

_____

3. Why are the Japanese people in America being removed?

_____

_____

4. Name a basic right affected by the removal of the Japanese-Americans.

_____

_____

The document involved here is a set of INSTRUCTIONS (capitalized words should been seen as hints) issued by the military to all Japanese people living in California. These instructions notify "all persons of Japanese ancestry" that they will be evacuated. So you should realize that the military is ordering the evacuation. Because the order affects "all Japanese persons, both alien and non-alien," you should realize that "alien" refers to those Japanese who are not U.S. citizens and "non-alien" refers to those Japanese who are American citizens. The third and fourth questions call for your use of outside historical knowledge. The order is dated 1942, so you should realize that the instructions were issued during World War II. Japanese people in America are being removed because the United States is at war with Japan following Japan's attack on Pearl Harbor. The civil rights of the Japanese were involved. Specifically, the rights of due process, which protects people's liberty and property, and equal protection under the law are involved.

DOCUMENT-BASED QUESTION POINTERS

For this part of the chapter, we focus our attention on the document-based question. Some of the pointers in this section explain the different characteristics of the documents that may be presented on the actual test. Other pointers offer advice on how to complete the written essay. Remember, Part III is worth 30 percent of your score (10 percent for the short answers and 20 percent for the essay). You will have 90 minutes to complete the tasks presented in this part.

General Pointers

> POINTER 1
>
> Read the entire direction sheet. It provides important information regarding the theme of the essay, the historical context, and what you are supposed to do.

The direction sheet gives you some very important information. The heading describes the time period and the theme. The general directions indicate the number of documents you will have to read in order to answer the questions (just like a constructed response question). There is a short statement giving you historical information about the theme. Then there is a description of the tasks you will be asked to complete (the actual written essay).

Listed on page 99 is an example of the document-based question section of the Grade Eight Intermediate Social Studies Test.

Part III: Document-Based Question
Part B—Essay
Generic Scoring Rubric

5

- Thoroughly addresses all aspects of the Task by accurately analyzing and interpreting at least four documents
- Incorporates information from the documents in the body of the essay
- Incorporates relevant outside information
- Richly supports the theme or problem with relevant facts, examples, and details
- Is a well-developed essay, consistently demonstrating a logical and clear plan of organization
- Introduces the theme or problem by establishing a framework that is beyond a simple restatement of the Task or
- Historical Context and concludes with a summation of the theme or problem

4

- Addresses all aspects of the Task by accurately analyzing and interpreting at least four documents
- Incorporates information from the documents in the body of the essay
- Incorporates relevant outside information
- Includes relevant facts, examples, and details, but discussion may be more descriptive than analytical
- Is a well-developed essay, demonstrating a logical and clear plan of organization
- Introduces the theme or problem by establishing a framework that is beyond a simple restatement of the Task or

- Historical Context and concludes with a summation of the theme or problem

3

- Addresses most aspects of the Task or addresses all aspects of the Task in a limited way, using some of the documents
- Incorporates some information from the documents in the body of the essay
- Incorporates limited or no relevant outside information
- Includes some facts, examples, and details, but discussion is more descriptive than analytical
- Is a satisfactorily developed essay, demonstrating a general plan of organization
- Introduces the theme or problem by repeating the Task or Historical Context and concludes by simply repeating the theme or problem

2

- Attempts to address some aspects of the Task, making limited use of the documents
- Presents no relevant outside information
- Includes few facts, examples, and details; discussion restates contents of the documents
- Is a poorly organized essay, lacking focus
- Fails to introduce or summarize the theme or problem

1

- Shows limited understanding of the Task with vague, unclear references to the documents
- Presents no relevant outside information
- Includes little or no accurate or relevant facts, details, or examples
- Attempts to complete the Task, but demonstrates a major weakness in organization
- Fails to introduce or summarize the theme or problem

0

- Fails to address the Task, is illegible, or is a blank paper

Theme: World War II: At Home and Abroad

Part III: Document-Based Question
Part B—Essay

This question is based on the accompanying documents (1–7). Some of these documents have been edited for the purpose of this task. This question is designed to test your ability to work with historical documents. As you analyze the documents, take into account both the source of each document and the author's point of view.

Directions: The document-based question consists of two parts. Be sure to put the booklet number at the top of each page. Use black or dark ink to answer the question.

Historical Context

After the bombing of Pearl Harbor by the Japanese on December 7, 1941, the United States entered World War II. The war took its toll on the American people both on the home front and the war front. At home there was rationing of supplies, and a wartime draft was needed. The war ended after Japan surrendered because the United States dropped an atomic bomb on Hiroshima and Nagasaki.

Task

Using information from the documents and your knowledge of social studies, answer the questions that follow each document in Part A. Your answers to the questions will help you write the Part B essay in which you will be asked to:

- Identify and discuss two reasons the United States entered the war
- Describe the impact of World War II on the home front
- Explain the impact the war had on Japanese-American citizens

Notice how you are told immediately that the historical time period deals with World War II. You also learn that you will have to answer questions about seven documents dealing with the theme of how the war was fought at home and abroad. What conditions did U.S. civilians face during the war? How did the United States respond to the Japanese attack on Pearl Harbor? You are given background information in the Historical Context.

Specifically, you are told that the war began after the attack on Pearl Harbor. In addition, the Historical Context establishes the fact that the government had to begin the rationing of supplies. And you are also given information about the draft needed to enlist soldiers to fight in the war. The task is the actual essay you will be expected to write. In this case, you must *identify* and *discuss two reasons* why the United States declared war on Japan. You are also asked to *describe* how World War II had an effect on people in the United States. And finally, you are asked to *explain* what happened to Japanese-American citizens during the war. The seven documents provided will help you with your answers.

POINTER 2

Look at the documents provided. The same hints you received for the constructed response section of Part II can also be used when answering the short answer document-based questions of Part III.

- Identify the type of document involved.
- Remember that you have a total of 90 minutes for the short answer questions and the essay.
- Be aware that a zero-to-one or one-to-two point scoring rubric will be used to score each of the questions.
- Take notes in the margin of the test book as you find valuable information in the documents.
- If the document is a reading passage, look for a point of view. Also look for vocabulary words that give you an idea as to what the passage is about.
- If the document is a cartoon, look for the point that the cartoonist is trying to make.
- If the document is a graph, look for the information being conveyed.
- If the document is a chart, identify the information provided.
- If there is a time component to the document, identify the time period and any events related to that time period.
- Look for hints in the document itself such as a key phrase or word.

- Study the different parts of a map and look for geographical and historical information.
- Note how the questions move from simple to more complex.
- If a question asks for examples from the document, make sure you keep your answers simple and straight to the point.
- If you find parts of the document too difficult to understand, pick out phrases that you do understand to get a better idea about its point of view and historical setting.

Let's take a look at the documents from Part A and apply these pointers to them.

Document 1: The Lend Lease Act (March 11, 1941)

Early in January 1941, President Roosevelt submitted to Congress an act designed to change the limitations imposed by previous neutrality legislation.

Be it enacted that this Act may be cited as "An act to Promote the Defense of the United States."

To sell, transfer title to, exchange, lease, lend, or otherwise dispose of, to any foreign government any defense article . . . Nothing in this act shall be construed (understood) to authorize or to permit the authorization of the entry of any American vessel into a combat area in violation of the Neutrality Act of 1939.

1a. What was the purpose of this law? (1)

The purpose of the law was to allow the United States to exchange or lend non-war goods to other countries, while keeping the United States out of the war.

1b. What condition was set forth in the law regarding American involvement in a combat zone? (1)

The United States was not allowed to send any vessel carrying goods into a combat zone because it would violate the Neutrality Act of 1939.

Document 2: "Rosie the Riveter"

© CORBIS

2a. What does the woman in the poster represent? (1)

<u>Women living in America during World War II.</u>

2b. Why was the woman referred to as "Rosie the Riveter"? (1)

<u>The women was called "Rosie the Riveter" because she worked in a factory during the war because of the shortage of men.</u>

Document 3: War Coupon Books

The War Production Board was another committee formed at the beginning of the war.

They were in charge of controlling or suspending the production of consumer goods.

Gas Coupon	Who Was Eligible	Value
A	General Population	4 gallons/week
B	Those who drove long distances	Pertains to how much they needed
C	Ministers, Doctors	Pertains to how much they needed
D	Motorcycles	2 gallons/week
E	Non-highway vehicles	2 gallons/week
R	Non-highway vehicles	5 gallons/week
TT	Approved commercial trucks	5 gallons/week
X	Congressmen, Politicians	Unlimited

3a. Explain the difference between Coupon A and Coupon X. (1)

Coupon A applied to the general population and allowed people 4 gallons of gas per week. Coupon X applied to Congressmen and politicians and gave them unlimited access to gasoline.

3b. What effect did the coupon system have on the home front? (1)

As a result of this coupon system, goods were rationed among people according to what they did for a living.

Document 4: Propaganda Posters

© CORBIS

© CORBIS

4a. How do these posters show propaganda? (1)

Poster 1 illustrates how people working side by side in a factory will contribute to victory. Poster 2 warns that the country is threatened by both Germany and Japan.

4b. Which poster displays racial or ethnic prejudice? Why? (1)

Poster 2 portrays the Japanese and Nazi in an unflattering manner in order to unite Americans.

Document 5: Map of Internment Camps

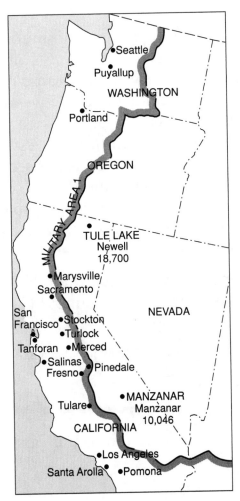

5a. What does the map indicate about the Japanese relocation? (1–2)

The map shows the area designated for the relocation of Japanese-American citizens such as Manzanar and Tule Lake.

Document 6: Supreme Court Decision in *Korematsu* v. *U.S.* (1944)

> All citizens alike, both in and out of uniform, feel the impact of war in greater or lesser measure . . . Korematsu was not excluded from the Military Area because of hostility to him or his race. He was excluded because we are at war with the Japanese Empire, because the properly constituted military authorities feared an invasion of our West Coast and felt constrained (forced) to take proper security measures, because they decided that the military urgency of the situation demanded that all citizens of Japanese ancestry be segregated from the West Coast temporarily . . .

6a. What did the Supreme Court say regarding the legality of putting Japanese-Americans into internment camps? (1)

The Supreme Court ruled that it was legal to assign Japanese-American citizens in internment camps during World War II.

6b. Give one reason behind the decision to put Japanese-American citizens into internment camps. (1)

According to the court, since there was a national emergency, a declared war, it was justified to order the Japanese-Americans into the camps.

Document 7: Interview with an Atomic Bomb Survivor

> **What happened to you when the explosion occurred?**
> When I saw a very strong light, a flash, I put my arms over my face unconsciously. Almost instantly I felt my face was inflating. I thought I was directly hit by the bomb and was dying. Shortly after, I felt my body flying in the air and then I lost consciousness.
>
> **What did you see after that?**
> When I was rescued, my hair was burned; my face was inflated like a balloon. Though my mother did not say, I knew it. I wondered why my shirt had been burnt and hanging around my arms, I soon realized they were pieces of my skin. It was hell. I saw people looking for water and they died soon after they drank it.

7a. Why was the Japanese woman so scared? (1)

She was scared because she was wounded so badly by the atomic bomb.

7b. What impact did this event have on World War II? (1)

The bomb forced Japan to surrender and end the war.

ESSAY POINTERS

Now let's look at the essay question and using general and specific pointers, develop a straightforward strategy for writing it.

Directions:

- Write a well-organized essay that includes an introduction, several paragraphs, and a conclusion.
- Use evidence from the documents to support your response.
- Include specific related outside information.
- Use black or dark ink to write your essay.

Historical Context

After the bombing of Pearl Harbor by the Japanese on December 7, 1941, the United States entered World War II. The war took its toll on the American people both on the home front and the war front. At home there was rationing of supplies and a wartime draft was needed.

Task

Using information from the documents and your knowledge of social studies, answer the questions that follow each document in Part A. Your answers to the questions will help you write the Part B essay in which you will be asked to:

- Identify and discuss two reasons the United States entered the war
- Describe the impact of World War II on the home front
- Explain the impact the war had on Japanese-American citizens

Be sure to include specific historical details. You must also include additional information from your knowledge of social studies.

Once you have reviewed the question carefully, and understand what you're being asked to do, use the pointers listed below. They will help you develop a plan for writing the best essay you can.

General Pointers

POINTER 1

Carefully read what you are being asked to do.

The document-based essay is very clear in what it is asking you to do. Let's break the question into its specific parts:

1. First you are told to use information from the seven documents you have already used to answer the short answer questions. If you have answered the questions in Part A, you will have the key elements needed for your essay.

2. The directions then tell you that you need an introduction, supporting paragraphs, and a conclusion. If you go back to the first part of the test and review the historical context, you will be on your way to

writing a solid introduction. Remember to rephrase the task in your own words. The supporting paragraphs should come directly from the documents that apply to what the essay is all about (**Document 1**: The Lend-Lease Act; **Document 2**: "Rosie the Riveter"; **Document 3**: The war coupon book; **Document 6**: The Supreme Court decision in *Korematsu*; and **Document 7**: An eyewitness account of an atomic bomb survivor). Your conclusion should sum up the main point of your essay.

3. In developing your supporting paragraphs, you are asked to identify, discuss, describe, and explain various items. It is very important that you understand what these words mean. "Identify" simply means to state reasons. "Discuss" means to present something in detail using facts, reasoning, and arguments. "Describe" means to illustrate something in words or to tell about it. And "explain" means to make plain, or to give reasons for.

POINTER 2

Be aware of time limits.

As a rule, you should be able to answer the short answer (scaffolding) questions in about 30 minutes and write the essay in about 45 minutes.

POINTER 3

Use scrap paper to pre-write your essay.

Create a "Boxed Document-Based Question Outline" (see page 110). Refer to the documents and the answers you gave in Part A. Pick out the most important information from the documents that apply to the essay. You should also make note of any additional information and historical examples that help you identify, discuss, describe, and explain your answer to the essay question.

Task	Introduction	Document Support of Task	Document Support of Task	Document Support of Task	Document Support of Task	Outside Information	Conclusion
A. Two reasons why U.S. entered the war. **B.** Impact of the war on the home front. **C.** Impact the war had on Japanese-American citizens.	On December 7, 1941, Japan attacked Pearl Harbor without warning and President Roosevelt asked Congress to declare war on the Axis powers. As a result, the attack had an impact on the home front.	*Number 1 supports Task A* The Allies had a difficult time defeating Germany. The Lend Lease Act was passed by Congress—it permitted the United States to lend and lease war materials to the Allies.	*Number 2 supports Task B* Because of the military draft, more women were needed to work in the factories. "Rosie the Riveter" illustrates the changing roles of women during World War II.	*Number 3 supports Task B* Rationing of gas and other materials created hardship for Americans who were not in the armed forces.	*Number 5 and 6 supports Task C* The map of Japanese-American internment camps and the *Korematsu* case illustrate the legality of the order and its impact on Japanese-Americans.	Japan attacked Pearl Harbor without warning, which caused the U.S. to declare war. The war eventually ended with the Allies meeting in Potsdam and Yalta.	World War II had a dramatic impact on the American people. They were forced to live under a system of rationing. Women took on a different role. Japanese-American citizens were forced to live in the internment camps.

Use the boxed outline to jot down an introduction, the relevant information from the documents, and a conclusion.

POINTER 4

After you pre-write your essay on the lined sheets of paper given to you, use your notes to write the essay in the test booklet. Use a pen and write neatly.

POINTER 5

Keep to the task and organize your ideas into a well-written essay.

The question asks you to write an introduction, so start your essay with a one-sentence opener. If you need to identify and discuss two reasons, only give two reasons. If the question calls on you to describe the impact, talk about a very important reason and if it calls for an explanation, give valid reasons.

POINTER 6

Underline the specific tasks that are given to you in the direction part of the essay (write an introduction, supporting paragraphs, and a conclusion) and the specific number of examples you must include.

POINTER 7

Understand and use the other essay pointers.

- Analyze: divide something into parts. Explain the meaning of each part.
- Compare and Contrast: show the similarities between ideas.
- Evaluate: give the positive and negative points about a subject.
- Summarize: repeat some of the main points you made in your essay.

POINTER 8

Use key words that show:

- Sequence: first, second, next, finally, in conclusion.
- Order of importance: most important, least important, major importance.
- Examples: for example, for instance.
- Comparison: if something is similar or different.
- Cause and Effect: therefore, as a result of, for this reason.

POINTER 9

If you have trouble with any of the documents, use examples and answers from the documents that you do understand.

Ideally, you will use the appropriate documents to help you answer each part of the essay. However, if you have trouble with one of the documents, make sure you use information from other documents in writing your essay.

POINTER 10

In addition to the documents, rely on your common historical knowledge.

Besides the information that you use from the documents, also include historical events. For instance in this essay, you can certainly use relevant information regarding the military draft and its impact on the home front, the fact that the United States was also involved in a war against Germany and Italy, and the decisions the United States had to make with regard to the Soviet Union's role in the war.

POINTER 11

Edit and proofread your essay. After you have completed your essay, the final step is to read it over and make any final changes. If you must cross out, do it neatly.

Let's apply these pointers to the document-based essay using a model essay that would have received a score of five. Just to remind you, here is the opening page of the DBQ again.

Theme: World War II: At Home and Abroad

Part III: Document-Based Question
Part B—Essay

This question is based on the accompanying documents (1–7). Some of these documents have been edited for the purpose of this task. This question is designed to test your ability to work with historical documents. As you analyze the documents, take into account both the source of each document and the author's point of view.

Directions: The document-based question consists of two parts. Be sure to put the booklet number at the top of each page. Use black or dark ink to answer the question.

Historical Context

After the bombing of Pearl Harbor by the Japanese on December 7, 1941, the United States entered World War II. The war took its toll on the American people both on the home front and the war front. At home there was rationing of supplies and a wartime draft was needed. The war ended after Japan surrendered because the United States dropped an Atomic bomb on Hiroshima and Nagasaki.

Task

Using information from the documents and your knowledge of social studies, answer the questions that follow each document in Part A. Your answers to the questions will help you write the Part B essay in which you will be asked to:

■ Identify and discuss two reasons the United States entered the war
■ Describe the impact of World War II on the home front
■ Explain the impact the war had on Japanese-American citizens

Now here is an essay that uses the pointers we just discussed.

On December 7, 1941 Japan attacked Pearl Harbor without warning and President Franklin Delano Roosevelt asked Congress to declare war on Japan, Germany and Italy. Immediately following the declaration of war the United States increased the pace of drafting men into the army. As a result, the war had a tremendous impact on the people living in the United States. The war also affected the Japanese-Americans living on the west coast.

Two reasons why the United States entered the war were because our European allies, England and France, were having a very difficult time defeating Germany even though we were helping them. And the United States also entered the war because Japan attacked Pearl Harbor without any warning. According to Document 1, The United States Congress passed the Lend Lease Act in 1941. This act permitted the United States to lend and lease materials to our allies even though our government was following a policy of neutrality. Even though we made this agreement with our allies, England and France, Germany was still able to conquer most of Europe by 1941. And then Japan surprised the United States with a sneak attack on the military base at Pearl Harbor in Hawaii. Without warning, the Japanese unleashed its air force and totally destroyed our naval base. Franklin Roosevelt called the attack "a day that will live in infamy" and Congress passed a declaration of war. A military draft began and the United States also declared war on Germany and Italy.

Because the United States had to fight a war in Europe against Germany and Italy and in the Pacific against Japan the country had to become totally united. It did this by transforming the economy to a wartime economy. According to Document 2, women had to work in factories in order to produce enough weapons and other materials that would help the military defeat Germany, Italy and Japan. These women were identified in a poster called "Rosie the Riveter." This meant that as men had to leave and join the military to fight the war, women went to work in factories. This was the first time in American history that so many women worked in factories. Another impact of the war on the home front was that the government had to ration goods. They did this because many goods were needed for the men in the armed forces fighting the war overseas. According to Document 3 the general population was only allowed four gallons of gasoline per week while more important people like approved commercial trucks and congressmen were allowed more gasoline. The reason for this was that gasoline was needed to help fight the war. There were also coupon books for food and clothing and people were also asked to support the war by purchasing war bonds. Posters were put up urging people to support the war effort.

Though there were many loyal Japanese-American citizens, the army asked President Roosevelt to issue an order relocating Japanese-Americans living on the west coast to internment camps. The map in document 5 shows where these camps were located. Two of the more notable camps were Manzamar and Tule Lake. Document 6 points out that many Japanese-Americans were upset when Roosevelt signed the order to relocate them to these camps. One person, Korematsu, refused to go to the camp and he was fined and sent to jail. He appealed his conviction, but the Supreme Court decided that in a time of national emergency like a war, the government had the right to take away the civil liberties of its citizens. Many people felt the decision was wrong especially since German-Americans and Italian-Americans were not sent to camps. After the war ended, in 1988, Congress voted to give money to the Japanese who were sent to these camps as a way of saying that the country was wrong.

The war ended in Europe before it ended in the Pacific. As a result of meetings in Potsdam and Yalta, the United States, Great Britain, France and the Soviet Union agreed to work together after the war ended in the Pacific. The Soviet Union felt that they could control Eastern Europe and also rule over East Germany and East Berlin. The United States ended the war with Japan by dropping two Atomic Bombs, one on Hiroshima and the other on Nagasaki. Eyewitness accounts in Document 7 illustrate the fear and confusion of the Japanese people as a result of these bombs.

World War Two had a dramatic impact on the American people. They were forced to live under a system of rationing, but were united against a common enemy. Women took on a different role, working in the factory while men were drafted into the war. Japanese American citizens were forced into internment camps and the Supreme Court ruled that these camps did not violate the Constitution. Ultimately the United States was victorious.

Chapter 5

Glossary of Terms, Historical Documents, and Key Court Decisions

GLOSSARY OF TERMS

Glossary terms are rated using an asterisk (*). One asterisk (*) indicates that the term is found on a test. Two asterisks (**) indicate that the term has been used on more than one exam.

**Abolition movement that favored the elimination of slavery through the passage of laws. People who favored the abolishment of slavery by legal means were called "Abolitionists."

Albany Plan of Union (1754) plan put forth by colonial leaders meeting at Albany, New York that sought to join the English colonies together under a president appointed by the king. The king rejected the plan.

amendment an addition or change to the Constitution. There are currently 27 amendments.

American Federation of Labor craft union of skilled workers organized by Samuel Gompers.

American Railway Union organized group of railroad laborers led by Eugene V. Debs. Debs organized a violent strike against railroad owners.

Annapolis Convention of 1786 meeting in Annapolis, Maryland where leaders from the different states urged a major revision of the Articles of Confederation.

Antifederalists those people who argued against the ratification (approval) of the Constitution.

anti-trust laws that place limitations on businesses designed to prevent the formation of monopolies (businesses that seek to eliminate competition).

***appeasement** policy followed by Great Britain and other European nations before the outbreak of World War II allowing Adolf Hitler to take land without opposition.

***archaeologist** a person who studies the past through relics.

***Articles of Confederation** the charter of the first national government of the United States. Its features included state governments that were more powerful than the central government and no elected president.

assembly line manufacturing process, developed by Henry Ford in the 1920s, whereby factory workers engage in specific and repetitive tasks.

***Aztecs** one of the first great empires of ancient America occupying central and southern Mexico between 1200 A.D. and 1400 A.D.

Berlin airlift (1949) the U.S. response to the Soviet Union's attempt to drive the United States and its allies out of West Berlin by blockading the city during the Cold War. It involved a massive airlift of food and other materials by the United States lasting over three months.

Berlin Wall the wall built by the East German government with the support of the Soviet Union in 1961 to prevent East German citizens from fleeing to the West.

bicameral legislature a legislative body made up of two houses.

big business term referring to those businesses that use outside resources, such as selling stock, to become large corporations.

Big Stick policy foreign policy developed by Theodore Roosevelt; it gave a message to Latin America that the United States would take a more active role in their affairs including use of military intervention.

***Bill of Rights** the first ten amendments to the Constitution; it guarantees basic rights to U.S. citizens and limits the government's ability to reduce basic liberties such as freedom of speech, the press, and religion, and the rights of the accused.

black codes laws passed by Southern states after the Civil War restricting the rights of freed slaves.

*Blitzkrieg military tactic developed by the Nazis during World War II involving a quick and decisive strike by armed forces.

Boston Massacre (1770) the killing of five colonists in Boston by British soldiers led by Captain Thomas Preston.

Boston Tea Party reaction of colonists in Boston against tea taxes imposed by the British. The colonists, dressed as Indians, boarded British ships and dumped tea into Boston Harbor.

*boycott tactic used to pressure a business into negotiations by urging consumers to stop dealing with or buying products from that business.

*_Brown_ v. _Board of Education_ (1954) landmark decision by the Supreme Court outlawing school segregation and reversing the _Plessy_ v. _Ferguson_ doctrine of "separate but equal."

budget a government's financial plan for raising and spending money.

cabinet the heads of executive departments of the U.S. government who advise the president. Created by George Washington, the cabinet is an example of the "unwritten constitution."

Camp David Accords agreements made between Egypt and Israel in which Egypt recognized Israel's independence; it was negotiated by President Jimmy Carter at the president's retreat home at Camp David.

*captains of industry term given to the heads of the big monopolies during the "Gilded Age." John D. Rockefeller, Cornelius Vanderbilt, and Andrew Carnegie are examples.

Carpetbaggers Northerners who packed their belongings and moved to the South after the Civil War to take government positions, and ended up running the governments of many Southern states.

census a counting of people. The Bureau of the Census does this every ten years, a requirement of the Constitution.

central government also known as the federal government; it is located in Washington, D.C.

*checks and balances principle of government that separates federal powers among three branches and prevents a single branch from becoming too powerful.

Citizen Genêt affair (1793) incident in which a French minister stirred up anti-British sentiment in the United States.

civil disobedience form of nonviolent protest used by people who refuse to obey a law with which they disagree.

civil rights basic privileges and liberties of citizens.

Clay's Compromise (1820) agreement arranged by Henry Clay that led to the Missouri Compromise, which determined the boundary between free and slave states.

*Cold War period following World War II and lasting until the downfall of the Soviet Union in 1991, characterized by competition between democratic and communist countries.

collective bargaining method by which workers negotiate with their employers through their union.

collective security treaty among countries designed to protect members from outside attack by agreeing that an attack on one country will be considered an attack on all.

colony a territory controlled by a more powerful country.

Compromise of 1850 law that established the boundary between free and slave territories and revised the Missouri Compromise.

*****Congress** the legislative or lawmaking body of the United States government made up of the Senate and the House of Representatives.

consent of the governed philosophy calling for the direct election of governmental representatives by the people. Once elected these lawmakers would respond to the policies favored by those who elected them.

*****Constitution** document that outlines the powers and limitations of the U.S. government.

Constitutional Convention (1787) meeting of delegates from the original thirteen states in Philadelphia for the purpose of revising the Articles of Confederation. Instead, the delegates drafted the Constitution.

*****containment** policy pursued by the United States during the Cold War to stop the spread of communism.

convention meeting of political delegates.

*****corporation** a business that sells stock in order to raise money.

*****court packing plan** attempt by President Franklin Roosevelt to increase the size of the Supreme Court in order to appoint members sympathetic to his policies; the proposal was rejected by Congress.

craft union labor union made up of a specific group of skilled workers, such as plumbers.

Credit Mobilier major scandal involving the bribery of Congressmen by a railroad construction company in return for government contracts during President Grant's administration.

*****creditor nation status** economic consequence resulting from a nation's ability to export more goods than it imports.

Cuban missile crisis military showdown between the United States and Soviet Union resulting from the U.S. discovery of Soviet missiles on Cuba. The military blockade of Cuba ordered by President Kennedy eventually led to the removal of the missiles.

culture the beliefs, values, and customs of a particular group or race of people.

*****Declaration of Independence** document written by Thomas Jefferson declaring the United States as an independent nation, and stating that all men have the basic rights of life, liberty, and the pursuit of happiness.

*deficit spending economic consequence that occurs when a government spends more money than it collects from taxes and other revenues.

delegated powers those powers listed in the Constitution that are not specifically reserved for the federal government.

democracy form of government characterized by free and open election of representatives who are responsive to the will of the people.

Democratic Party one of the two major political parties in the United States today. Its symbol is the donkey.

Democratic-Republicans one of first political parties formed in the United States. Thomas Jefferson was one of the party's leaders.

depression economic downturn characterized by high unemployment, low production, and numerous business failures.

desegregation policy designed to end the "separate but equal" doctrine by allowing equal access to all races.

détente policy favored by President Nixon, and later President Reagan, resulting in a lessening of hostilities between the Soviet Union and the United States.

direct election of senators result of the Seventeenth Amendment, adopted in 1913, giving people the right to vote for their senators.

disarmament policy that favors the reduction of nuclear weapons.

dollar diplomacy type of foreign policy by which a country invests money in a foreign government for the purpose of influencing that nation's affairs; the United States pursued this policy in Latin America during the early twentieth century.

domino theory Cold War belief that as one nation fell to the communists, neighboring nations would follow. For example, if South Vietnam were taken over by North Vietnam, the communists would also conquer other nations in Southeast Asia.

Dred Scott v. *Sanford* (1857) case in which the Supreme Court decided that slaves were property; the decision was a catalyst for the Civil War.

due process of law principle in the Constitution that provides a person accused of a crime with procedures guaranteeing a fair trial.

Dust Bowl Midwestern states suffering from a drought that prevented farmers from growing crops and forced many to leave their farms during the Great Depression.

*elastic clause section of the Constitution enabling the government to make any laws "necessary and proper" to carry out its specific powers. It is also known as the "necessary and proper clause."

**electoral college established by the Founding Fathers, it is a method of indirectly electing the president and vice president by a delegation of electors from each state. The number of electors a state has is equal to the number of Senators and House members the state has in Congress.

*Emancipation Proclamation (1863) President Lincoln's order freeing the slaves in the Southern states that seceded from the Union during the Civil War.

embargo order blocking goods of a particular country from entering into another country.

Enlightenment era during the seventeenth and eighteenth centuries in which philosophers like Locke, Hobbes, and Montesquieu believed in individual thought and natural rights of people.

equal protection under the law constitutional principle guaranteeing all people equal treatment under the law; it was made applicable to the citizens of every state through the Fourteenth Amendment.

*Erie Canal canal connecting New York City with Buffalo along Lake Erie, completed in 1825. The canal opened new markets from New York City to Albany, and Albany to Buffalo.

Espionage Act of 1917 law making it illegal to interfere with the operations of the U.S. armed forces, including the recruitment of soldiers through a draft.

ethnocentrism belief that a person's own ethnic group is superior to others.

executive branch branch of government, headed by the president, that carries out the laws of the land.

*federalism form of government that divides power between a central government and state governments.

federal reserve system established by Congress in 1913, the system regulates the nation's money supply through policies established by an independent board of governors.

Federalists people who favored ratification of the Constitution and a powerful central government. They wrote the *Federalist Papers*, which outlined reasons for approving the Constitution. Federalists included Alexander Hamilton and James Madison.

Fifteenth Amendment (1870) an amendment passed after the Civil War giving freed slaves the right to vote.

*First Continental Congress (1774) meeting of representatives of all colonies, except Georgia, in Philadelphia, in response to the Intolerable Acts imposed on the colonists by Great Britain.

forced removals forced resettlement of Indian nations authorized by President Andrew Jackson. One such removal of tribes from Georgia became known as the "Trail of Tears" because of the number of Native Americans who died along the march westward.

foreign policy the manner in which a country conducts itself with other countries; it is usually based on national security interests.

*Fourteen Points Woodrow Wilson's plan for world peace after WW I, which included creation of the League of Nations. The League of Nations was adopted as part of the terms of the Treaty of Versailles.

Fourteenth Amendment (1868) one of the amendments passed after the Civil War; it granted freed slaves citizenship and guaranteed all citizens equal protection under the law.

freedman a freed slave; usually refers to a slave freed by the Thirteenth Amendment.

freedom of religion one of the rights guaranteed by the First Amendment and contained in the Bill of Rights. It includes the freedom to practice religion without government interference and requires the separation of church and state by prohibiting the government from establishing a national religion.

freedom of speech one of the rights guaranteed by the First Amendment and contained in the Bill of Rights. It allows individuals and groups the right to express their views without government interference.

freedom of the press one of the rights guaranteed by the First Amendment and contained in the Bill of Rights. It guarantees individuals and groups the right to publish printed material without government interference.

frontier border region between settled and unsettled territories.

frontier thesis Frederick Jackson Turner's belief that democracy spreads westward as the frontier moves westward.

Fugitive Slave Law (1850) act of Congress requiring Northern states to return escaped slaves to their Southern owners; rewards were often given for their return.

Gilded Age phrase used by Mark Twain to describe the extravagant and often corrupt life styles of wealthy U.S. business tycoons in the late 1800s.

global interdependence refers to the economic relationship between countries and the growing need for free trade, such as elimination of trade barriers, in order to improve economic conditions throughout the world.

Good Neighbor policy foreign policy announced by President Franklin Roosevelt in 1933 to promote better relations with Latin America.

government organizational structure by which a country establishes rule by laws.

Granger movement (1867) founded by Oliver Kelly, it was a movement by farmers seeking to reform the railroad industry; officially called the National Grange of the Patrons of Husbandry.

Great Compromise agreement made at the Constitutional Convention of 1787 creating the two houses of Congress; one house based on population and the other house based on equal representation.

**Great Depression name given to the period between the stock market crash of 1929 and the start of World War II to describe the worst economic downturn in U.S. history; marked by reduced industrial production, business failures, and, at its height, an unemployment rate of 25 percent.

Great Society name given to the social welfare programs of President Lyndon Johnson designed to help the less fortunate; programs included Medicare, Head Start, and food stamps.

Hamilton's economic plan policy developed by Alexander Hamilton, as Secretary of the Treasury, to pay off the nation's war debt and improve the country's credit.

*Harlem Renaissance movement of black writers, artists, and musicians to Harlem, New York, marking a rebirth of black culture during the 1920s.

Haymarket Riot (1886) strike by workers at a Chicago factory that turned violent when a bomb exploded and killed several police officers attempting to break up the strike and police fired into the crowd.

**Holocaust mass murder of millions of European Jews and other minorities by the Nazis during World War II.

Homestead Act (1862) act of Congress giving free land to Western settlers if they maintained and improved the land for five years.

*House of Burgesses legislative body of the Virginia colony; it was the first elected representative legislature in the English colonies.

House of Representatives one of the two houses of Congress; its members are elected every two years and allotted among the states according to population.

hyphenated-Americans term given to the different ethnic, racial, and religious groups that came to the United States as immigrants and later became citizens. Examples include Irish-Americans; Asian-Americans, and Jewish-Americans.

immigration movement of people from one country to another; major causes of immigration include religious and political persecution and poverty.

impeachment process of bringing formal charges of misconduct against a public official for the purpose of removing the official from office.

*imperialism practice pursued by a country seeking an empire through possession of foreign territories or colonies.

inauguration ceremonial swearing-in and oath of office taken by an elected official at the beginning of his term.

Incas one of the earliest ancient American civilizations, founded in 1100 A.D. in Peru; by the time of their conquest by Spanish explorers in the 1500s, the Incas had established a powerful empire.

industrialization economic transformation of a country marked by development of large industries, mass production of goods, and reduction in its agricultural workforce.

*Industrial Revolution period of rapid economic development, beginning in the late eighteenth century, marked by mass-produced factory goods, and a reduced agrarian labor force.

Industrial Workers of the World labor union formed in 1905, its membership consisted of both skilled and unskilled laborers; members were known as "Wobblies."

initiative process for direct voter involvement in the making of laws through petition, referendum, and so on.

integration as applied to African-Americans, the bringing together of the races resulting from the end of the "separate but equal" doctrine; integration allowed African-Americans access to public facilities that were previously only open to whites.

internment as applied to Japanese-Americans, the forced relocation of U.S. citizens of Japanese descent during World War II.

Intolerable Acts series of harsh laws imposed by the British on the American colonies to assert control and raise revenues.

Iron Curtain term used by Winston Churchill to describe the border between Western Europe and Soviet-dominated Eastern Europe after World War II.

Iroquois one of the most powerful Native American nations in the eastern woodlands of New York State.

*__Iroquois Confederacy__ league of tribes of the Iroquois nation located in New York State; the Iroquois Confederacy sided with the British and helped defeat the French in the French and Indian War.

Jacksonian Democracy term used to describe the presidency of Andrew Jackson, characterized by greater political participation for the common man.

Jim Crow laws laws passed by Southern states after the Civil War enforcing segregation of the races.

judicial review principle established in *Marbury* v. *Madison;* the power of the Supreme Court to declare laws unconstitutional.

judiciary branch of government responsible for interpreting laws; the court system.

Kansas-Nebraska Act (1854) law allowing the people of Kansas and Nebraska to choose whether their territory would be admitted to the Union as a free or slave state.

Kellogg-Briand Pact of 1928 agreement outlawing the use of armed force to settle international disputes. The treaty lacked any enforcement capability.

Knights of Labor organized in 1869, an early labor union made up of skilled and unskilled workers.

Korean War (1950–1953) armed conflict resulting from communist North Korea's invasion across the Thirty-eighth parallel into South Korea. North Korea was supported by China; South Korea was supported by the United Nations. The United States sent troops as part of the U.N.'s police action.

*__Ku Klux Klan__ white supremacist organization founded after the Civil War, in response to Reconstruction, to intimidate freed slaves. It now opposes Jews and other minorities. Also known as the "KKK."

laissez-faire literally means "hands-off"; business principle advocating an economy free of governmental business regulations.

*__League of Nations__ international organization formed after World War I as part of the Treaty of Versailles to promote world peace. The Senate refused to allow the United States to join.

legislature branch of government responsible for making laws.

Lend-Lease Act (1941) act passed by Congress allowing President Franklin Roosevelt to lend or lease war materials to America's allies while keeping the United States neutral during the first years of World War II.

limited government belief that government power is restrained or limited by legal principles.

Louisiana Purchase (1803) agreement made by Thomas Jefferson to purchase the territory between the Mississippi River and the Rocky Mountains from France. The purchase more than doubled the size of the United States.

*****Loyalists** colonists who remained loyal to England during the Revolutionary War.

Magna Carta (1215) agreement signed by King John I guaranteeing certain rights to the people of England. Also known as the "Great Charter," it became the foundation of the Bill of Rights.

Manhattan Project secret project carried out in New Mexico that developed the atomic bomb during World War II.

*****Manifest Destiny** belief held by many Americans during the nineteenth century that it was God's will for the United States to expand its borders from the East Coast to the West Coast.

Marbury v. *Madison* (1803) Supreme Court decision written by Chief Justice John Marshall declaring a congressional act unconstitutional; the decision established the principle of judicial review.

*****March on Washington** (1963) gathering of over 500,000 people in front of the Lincoln Memorial urging Congress to pass civil rights legislation and where Reverend Martin Luther King, Jr., delivered his famous "I Have a Dream" speech. President Lyndon Johnson signed the Civil Rights Act of 1964 into law the following year.

Marshall Plan (1948–1951) program of massive U.S. financial aid designed to strengthen the economic, political, and social structures of European countries after World War II; developed by Secretary of State George Marshall. The goal of the plan was to prevent the spread of communism.

Maya early civilization located in southern Mexico and Central America; by 1000 B.C. the Maya had established an advanced culture.

*****Mayflower Compact** (1620) agreement among the Pilgrims to create a representative form of government in their new colony.

*****McCarthyism** term used to describe the search for communists and communist sympathizers within the United States during the 1950s; named after Senator Joseph McCarthy, who held hearings in an attempt to identify accused communists and sympathizers. McCarthy also alleged that there were communists inside the government. Many of the people who testified before the committee refused to answer questions by using their Fifth Amendment right against self-incrimation. Some were later black-listed, preventing future employment.

melting pot theory notion that immigrants blend into and contribute to the culture of their new country.

*****mercantilism** economic principle favoring the acquisition of colonies as a source of raw materials for and a market for finished goods of the mother country.

Mexican War (1846–1848) armed conflict between Mexico and the United States resulting in the U.S. acquisition of territory in Texas and the purchase of California and New Mexico for $15 million.

Miranda rights constitutional rights established by the Supreme Court in *Miranda* v. *Arizona* (1966), guaranteeing the criminally accused the right to remain silent, the right to an attorney, and the right to be informed that anything they say can be held against them.

Missouri Compromise (1820) agreement between advocates and opponents of slavery admitting Missouri as a slave state, Maine as a free state, and establishing a boundary between free territory and slave territory.

monopoly exclusive control or ownership of an industry by a single business with the purpose of reducing competition.

Monroe Doctrine (1823) policy announced by President James Monroe declaring the Western Hemisphere off limits to European colonial powers.

*****Montgomery Bus Boycott** (1955) year-long refusal of black citizens of Montgomery, Alabama to ride the public bus system as a result of the arrest of Rosa Parks, a black woman who did not give up her seat to a white man.

*****muckrakers** American journalists who wrote investigative reports during the Progressive Era, exposing the ills of society and calling for government reform of political, social, and economic institutions.

National Association for the Advancement of Colored People (NAACP) organization advocating greater equality for African-Americans through peaceful means, founded in 1910.

Native Americans original inhabitants of North America.

*****nativism** policy opposing immigration to the United States; nativists favored quotas.

natural rights liberties granted by God to which all people are entitled as human beings; first discussed by John Locke, these rights include life, liberty, and property.

necessary and proper clause section of the Constitution granting Congress the right to make any laws "necessary and proper" for carrying out any of its stated powers; also known as the "elastic" clause.

neutrality foreign policy statement of a nation refusing to help either side of a war.

*****New Deal** legislation developed by President Franklin Roosevelt using the power of the federal government to create relief, recovery, and reform programs to combat the Great Depression.

New England geographic region of the United States bounded by Maine in the north and Rhode Island in the south.

New France early French colonial settlement in North America; it eventually led to further colonization in America in the seventeenth century.

New Netherlands Dutch colonial settlement in New York founded by Peter Minuit in 1625.

New Spain Spanish colonial settlements in America founded by Christopher Columbus in 1492, it included settlements in North, Central, and South America.

*****Nineteenth Amendment** (1920) constitutional amendment giving women the right to vote.

North American Free Trade Agreement (NAFTA) agreement passed by Congress in 1994 eliminating trade barriers between the United States, Canada, and Mexico.

North Atlantic Treaty Organization (NATO) military alliance between the United States and democratic nations of Western Europe formed in 1949 in response to the Soviet Union's influence over Eastern Europe. Its aim was the collective security of member nations, declaring that an attack on one nation would be considered to be an attack on all the nations in NATO.

Northwest Ordinance of 1787 legislation providing for the admission of the Northwest Territory to the Union and its administration; the Ordinance prohibited slavery in the newly admitted states and granted admission on an equal basis with the thirteen original states.

Nullification Act (1828) laws enacted by Southern states allowing a state to overrule or nullify a law of the federal government on the basis that Congress had exceeded its powers.

Open Door policy foreign policy doctrine announced in 1899 in an attempt to preserve U.S. trade with China by requesting European powers to respect China's sovereignty and permitting free access to Asian ports.

patroonship system manner in which land was organized by Dutch settlers in New Netherlands.

Peace Corps (1961) federal program designed to aid developing countries by sending U.S. volunteers to teach and provide assistance; founded by President John F. Kennedy.

*****Pearl Harbor** Hawaiian naval station attacked, without warning, by the Japanese on December 7, 1941. The attack resulted in a U.S. declaration of war against Japan, Germany, and Italy.

Persian Gulf War (1991) armed conflict between Iraq and coalition of U.N. troops, led by the United States, after Iraqi leader Saddam Hussein's invasion of neighboring Kuwait; Iraq was quickly defeated.

Pinckney Treaty (1795) U.S. agreement with Spain settling land disputes between the two countries after the Revolutionary War.

plantation system method of land management practiced in the South utilizing slave labor and overseers (individuals in charge of slave labor).

Plessy v. *Ferguson* (1896) Supreme Court decision establishing the "separate but equal" doctrine, making segregation legal.

poll tax tax paid by individuals wishing to vote enacted by Southern states in an attempt to prevent freed slaves from exercising their right to vote; poll taxes were made unconstitutional by the Twenty-fourth Amendment.

pools illegal agreements made between railroad companies operating in the same geographic location limiting the number of companies and reducing competition.

*****populism** political movement of the late 1800s favoring greater government regulation of business, a graduated income tax, and greater political involvement by the people.

Preamble introduction to the Constitution stating the purposes of the document; begins with "We the people, in order to form a more perfect union . . ."

president head of the executive branch of government.

primary election election that determines a political party's nominee for political office.

*****primary source document** first hand account of an historical event; eyewitness accounts are one example.

*Progressive Era (1900–1920) period characterized by political, economic, and social reform movements.

progressive tax method of taxation by which the amount of tax increases as the amount a person earns increases; made legal by the Sixteenth Amendment.

**Prohibition (1919–1933) period of time from enactment of the Eighteenth Amendment, making the sale, production, and transportation of alcohol illegal, through its repeal by the Twenty-first Amendment.

protective tariff (1828) tax on imported goods designed to protect domestic industries by increasing prices of imports. In the South, protective tariffs were disliked as European countries placed retaliatory tariffs on Southern goods like cotton.

Pure Food and Drug Act (1906) Progressive Era law regulating the sale of meat and prescription drugs; the legislation was instigated by the writings of muckrakers.

Puritans group of early English settlers who came to America to escape religious persecution.

Quakers group of early English settlers who established a colony in Pennsylvania. Quakers oppose war on religious grounds.

Quebec Act (1774) act of British government extending the boundaries of the Canadian Province of Quebec. The Quebec Act angered English colonists by threatening the territorial claims of the colonies.

Quota Act of 1924 series of laws limiting the number of immigrants allowed to enter the United States.

*ratification approval of a document or treaty.

recall election Progressive Era reform allowing voters to remove an office-holder from office before the end of his term.

*Reconstruction period from 1865 through 1876, when former Confederate states were occupied by federal troops and controlled by the national government prior to their re-admission to the Union.

Red Scare refers to periods marked by fear of communist invasion in the United States during the 1920s and the 1950s.

referendum Progressive Era reform giving people the right to vote directly for laws before they go into effect.

"Remember the *Maine*" headline from William Randolph Hearst's newspaper reporting the sinking of the *U.S.S. Maine* in Havana Harbor and suggesting that it was a result of a Spanish mine. It became the rallying cry of those who wanted war with Spain.

Republican Party one of the two major U.S. political parties. Founded in 1854, its first major political figure was Abraham Lincoln; its symbol, the elephant.

reserved powers powers not specifically granted by the Constitution to the federal government and held to be reserved to the states. Listed in the Tenth Amendment, they include the power of state governments to regulate education, maintain police, and guarantee the health and welfare of their citizens.

return to normalcy theme of President Warren G. Harding's administration; referring to a return to U.S. isolationism and increased economic expansion after World War I.

rights of the accused due process rights of the criminally accused, including the right against self-incrimination, the right to counsel, and the "Miranda rights."

*****Roaring Twenties** term used to describe the 1920s, characterized by an emerging middle class, increased factory production, rising prosperity, and changing social values.

robber barons term given to the great industrialists of the nineteenth century who used their money and power for their own purposes.

Roosevelt Corollary to the Monroe Doctrine foreign policy initiated by President Theodore Roosevelt asserting the right of the United States to act as "policeman" of the Western Hemisphere and to interfere in Latin American affairs.

"Rosie the Riveter" character from a World War II propaganda poster used to illustrate the increased need for women as factory workers.

salutary neglect term describing English colonists' belief that the British government's lack of interest in the colonies resulted in their ability to develop political and economic systems with little interference from England.

*****secession** withdrawal of Southern states from the Union in 1860.

secondary source document historical account reported by somebody who was not an eyewitness to the event.

sectionalism development of rivalries and alliances within the same country based on geographic or economic differences. Sectionalism created conflicts between the North and South and ultimately led to the Civil War.

Sedition Act of 1918 law limiting the right of individuals to publish articles criticizing U.S. policies in times of war.

segregation separation of the races; principle established by the doctrine of "separate but equal." Segregation resulted in the establishment of separate facilities for whites and blacks.

Senate the upper house of Congress; based on equal representation of two members from each state.

*****Seneca Falls Convention** (1848) convention held in Seneca Falls, New York for the purpose of furthering the rights of women; organized by Elizabeth Cady Stanton and Lucretia Mott. The convention issued the "Declaration of Sentiments," urging passage of legislation granting women more rights.

separate but equal doctrine established by the Supreme Court in *Plessy* v. *Ferguson* that allowed states to create separate facilities for blacks and whites.

separation of church and state principle established by the First Amendment prohibiting the government from establishing a religion and guaranteeing the people the right to freely exercise religious beliefs.

separation of powers principle of government established by the Constitution dividing governmental powers among three branches of government and assuring liberty through a system of checks and balances.

*****Seventeenth Amendment** (1918) constitutional amendment providing for the direct election of senators by the people. The amendment ended the previous method of appointment by state legislatures.

Shays' Rebellion (1786) armed rebellion in Massachusetts led by Daniel Shays to protest government auctions of farms for failure to pay to taxes.

Sherman Anti-trust Act (1890) law making it illegal for companies to "restrain trade" by eliminating competition. The act, aimed at eliminating monopolies, was initially ineffective as court decisions were favorable to businesses.

slavery act of holding persons against their will for involuntary servitude. Slavery was abolished by the Thirteenth Amendment.

Social Security Act (1935) New Deal legislation giving retired people economic security through payments made by the government.

Spanish American War (1898) armed conflict between Spain and the United States; resulting in Spain's defeat after three months and expansion of U.S. territorial rights in Cuba, the Philippines, and Puerto Rico.

Sputnik (1957) first unmanned space satellite launched by the Soviet Union.

Stamp Act (1765) British law imposing a tax, in the form of stamps, on all legal and printed documents used in the English colonies.

states' rights doctrine supporting the power of states to overrule, oppose, or withdraw from the federal government if they choose. Southern states believed in states' rights and eventually seceded from the Union prior to the Civil War; a direct cause of the Civil War.

stock margin credit used to purchase stock; difference between a stock's price and amount actually paid by purchaser. Margin amounts were limited as a result of the stock market crash of 1929.

*strike labor union tactic designed to force employers into making concessions through a work stoppage by employees.

suburb residential area located on the outskirts of a city.

*suffrage the right to vote.

supremacy clause contained in Article VI of the Constitution, the clause declaring the Constitution as "the supreme law of the land."

*Supreme Court highest court in the federal judicial branch of government; the Court rules on issues related to the Constitution.

Tammany Hall reference to New York City Democratic headquarters of the late nineteenth century and corrupt politicians, called "bosses," who controlled city government.

**tariff tax on imported goods.

Temperance movement founded by the Women's Christian Temperance Union seeking legislation designed to limit alcohol consumption.

third party political party other than Democrats and Republicans; movements that generally have a few issues as their driving force. The Populist Party of the late 1880s is an example.

Thirteenth Amendment (1865) constitutional amendment abolishing slavery in the United States.

three branches of government legislative, executive, and judicial branches of the federal government.

**Three-Fifths Compromise clause contained in the Constitution counting every five slaves as three people for purposes of calculating representation in Congress; reached at the Constitutional Convention in Philadelphia in 1787.

Tories English colonists sympathetic or loyal to the British during the Revolutionary War; also known as Loyalists.

*trade deficit economic consequence resulting from a nation's inability to export more goods than it imports.

Trail of Tears term used by Native Americans to describe forced removal of tribes after President Andrew Jackson's signing of the Indian Removal Act into law.

*__Transcontinental Railroad__ joining together of the Central Pacific and the Union Pacific Railroads at Promontory Point, Utah, in 1869, completing a route between the East and West Coasts.

**__Treaty of Paris__ (1783) agreement ending the American Revolution and granting the English colonies their independence.

triangular trade system of trade pursued by New England merchants in the late eighteenth and early nineteenth centuries that involved trading sugar, molasses, rum, finished goods, and slaves between the West Indies, Europe, and Africa.

Truman Doctrine (1947) foreign policy announcement by President Harry Truman providing economic and military assistance to nations threatened by invasion; it was a direct attempt to combat the Soviet Union's efforts to become more influential in Greece and Turkey.

*__trust__ combination of businesses joining together to limit competition within an industry; an industry-wide monopoly.

Tweed Ring organization founded by William Tweed, as head of New York City's Democratic Party during the late nineteenth century, using corrupt practices to gain political influence and profits.

Uncle Tom's Cabin (1852) book written by Abolitionist author, Harriet Beacher Stowe, describing the cruel treatment of black slaves in the South.

unconstitutional actions declared illegal due to their violation of the principles of the Constitution.

Underground Railroad system of assistance designed to aid fugitive slaves in their attempts to escape from Southern masters.

Union states that opposed secession during the Civil War.

United Nations Universal Declaration of Human Rights (1948) U.N. document stating the rights entitled to all citizens of the world.

unwritten Constitution policies and practices of government not specifically established by the Constitution but based on custom. Examples include the establishment of the president's cabinet and the formation of political parties.

*__Versailles Treaty__ (1919) peace agreement ending World War I; it included major parts of President Woodrow Wilson's "Fourteen Points," including establishment of the League of Nations. The treaty, which treated

Germany harshly, was rejected by the U.S. Senate after a bitter battle between President Wilson and Senate leader, Henry Cabot Lodge.

*veto power of the president to prevent enactment of a law passed by Congress. A presidential veto can be overridden by a two-thirds vote of Congress.

Vietnam War (1965–1975) undeclared war fought by the United States to prevent the fall of South Vietnam to invading forces from communist North Vietnam; the war ended with the withdrawal of U.S. troops after forces from North Vietnam captured South Vietnam's capital of Saigon. More than 50,000 U.S. troops were killed during the conflict.

Wagner Act (1935) act establishing the National Labor Relations Board and outlawing certain employer practices against labor as unfair; also known as the National Labor Relations Act.

War of 1812 armed conflict between the United States and Great Britain instigated by "War Hawks" elected to Congress who wanted western lands controlled by the British. The war ended with neither side claiming victory.

War Powers Act (1973) law limiting the president's power to use armed forces in combat without congressional approval.

Warsaw Pact collective security agreement between the Soviet Union and Eastern European satellite nations formed in response to the establishment of NATO.

Watergate term used in reference to the biggest political scandal in U.S. history; named for the Washington, D.C. hotel where the Democratic Party's national headquarters were broken into by supporters of President Nixon. The scandal eventually led to President Nixon's resignation.

Whigs political party, in existence from 1800 until the Civil War, that opposed the two major parties of the time; many members eventually joined the Republican Party.

Whiskey Rebellion (1794) armed rebellion by settlers in Pennsylvania and Virginia protesting a tax on whiskey passed as part of Treasury Secretary Alexander Hamilton's financial plan. Federal troops, under George Washington, put down the uprising.

*World War I (1916–1919) armed conflict, fought primarily in Europe, sparked by the assassination of Austrian Archduke Ferdinand and the resulting involvement of European military alliances. The United States entered the war in 1917 to "make the world safe for democracy" and, partially, in response to Germany's practice of unrestricted submarine warfare and the sinking of the *Lusitania.*

***World War II** (1939–1945) armed conflict starting in Europe with Hitler's invasion of Poland in 1939 and, eventually, spreading throughout most other regions of the world. The United States entered the war in 1941 on the side of the Allies after Japan bombed the U.S. naval base at Pearl Harbor, Hawaii. The war in Europe ended with Germany's surrender after the capture of Berlin; Japan's surrender after the United States dropped two atomic bombs marked the end of the war in Asia.

Yalta Conference (1945) last wartime meeting of the Allied leaders, in Yalta, outlining the organization of Europe in anticipation of Germany's defeat and the eventual end of World War II. The conference divided Germany and Berlin into zones of occupation and established the framework for the United Nations.

yellow journalism sensational, irresponsible, or misleading news as reported by the media for purposes of attracting viewers and provoking emotional public reaction.

Zimmerman Note (1917) message intercepted by the United States revealing Germany's plan to urge Mexico to attack the United States during World War I.

HISTORICAL DOCUMENTS

Listed below are historical documents that you should recognize. They include writings, speeches, political cartoons, books, poems, songs, and pieces of art significant to U.S. history. Some of these documents are important in their own right while others are important because of what they represent or say about the time in which they were created. These historical documents may be the subject of exam questions, particularly document-based questions, so review the list carefully and learn the significance of each. The documents listed below are identified by unit (Roman numeral) and standard (Arabic numeral).

The documents are rated using a plus sign (+). One plus sign (+) indicates that the document is found in the constructed response or document-based question section of a test. Two plus signs (++) indicate that the document is used in more than one part of an exam.

"The Marine Hymn" (Songs from World War I) VIII-1

Franklin Roosevelt's first inaugural address (1933) IX-1, 3, 5

Franklin Roosevelt's fireside chats IX-1, 5

Selections from *The Grapes of Wrath* IX-4

Hard Times (Studs Turkel) IX-4

"Brother, Can You Spare a Dime?" (song) IX-4

+Western Union telegraph to Franklin Roosevelt from Japanese-American citizens X-1, 3, 5

United States military recruitment posters X-1

+"Rosie the Riveter" poster X-1

"God Bless America," "This Land Is Your Land," and "Praise the Lord and Pass the Ammunition" (songs) X-1

United Nations Charter X-2

Gulf of Tonkin Resolution XI-1, 3, 5

"Where Have All the Flowers Gone?" (song) XI-1

Speech by Dr. Martin Luther King, Jr., at the Lincoln Memorial (1963) XI-1

John F. Kennedy's inaugural speech XI-1, 5

"We Shall Overcome" (song) XI-1

KEY COURT DECISIONS

Listed below, in chronological order, are some key court decisions that have affected U.S. history. Students should be familiar with the names of cases as well as with the legal principles set forth in these decisions as they may be the subject of test questions.

Trial of John Peter Zenger (1735) colonial era decision establishing the groundwork for freedom of the press.

Marbury v. *Madison* (1803) Supreme Court decision establishing the principle of judicial review.

Dred Scott v. *Sanford* (1857) Supreme Court decision declaring slaves to be property with no rights of citizenship.

Plessy v. *Ferguson* (1896) Supreme Court decision establishing the doctrine of "separate but equal."

Schenck v. *United States* (1919) Supreme Court decision limiting the rights of free speech and freedom of the press in situations where such freedoms would create a "clear and present danger."

Korematsu v. *United States* (1944) Supreme Court decision stating that civil liberties can be restricted during wartime.

Brown v. *Board of Education of Topeka* (1954) Supreme Court decision invalidating the "separate but equal" doctrine.

Engle v. *Vitale* (1962) Supreme Court decision finding prayer in public schools to be in violation of the separation between church and state.

Gideon v. *Wainwright* (1964) Supreme Court decision establishing the right of the criminally accused to an attorney even if the accused could not afford one.

Miranda v. *Arizona* (1966) Supreme Court decision establishing the Miranda rights; these direct police to inform the criminally accused of their right to remain silent, that anything said could be used against them, the right to an attorney, and the right to have an attorney appointed if the accused could not afford one.

Tinker v. *Des Moines Independent School District* (1969) Supreme Court decision establishing that students' constitutional rights do not stop at the "schoolhouse gates."

New York Times v. *United States* (1971) Supreme Court decision declaring that newspapers can print sensitive stories dealing with war as long as they do not violate national security; also known as the "Pentagon Papers" case.

Roe v. *Wade* (1973) Supreme Court decision asserting that the right to an abortion is constitutionally protected.

United States v. *Nixon* (1974) Supreme Court decision establishing the principle that the president is not above the law.

Model Examinations and Answers

MODEL EXAMINATION 1

The core of Model Examination 1 has been provided courtesy of Eastern Suffolk BOCES and Dr. Robert Bedford, Supervisor of Instructional Support Planning and Technology Services.

PART I: MULTIPLE-CHOICE

Directions (1-45)

Each question is followed by four choices. Read each question carefully. Decide which choice is the correct answer. Mark your answer in the space provided.

1. Why did Spain set up colonies in the New World?

    1. to set up a fur-trading industry
    2. to establish homes for people from Spain
    3. to capture slaves to sell to other countries
    4. to protect its claims on New World land and wealth

    1. _____

2. Which products were most important to the Southern colonies?

    1. iron and copper
    2. tobacco, indigo, and rice
    3. fish and lumber
    4. barley, corn, and rye

    2. _____

3. The New York State Constitution and the United States Constitution both provide for

   1. a federal system of government.
   2. an electoral college.
   3. a two-house legislative branch.
   4. elections every six years.

   3. _____

4. Use your knowledge of social studies and the description of how a tariff works to answer the following question.

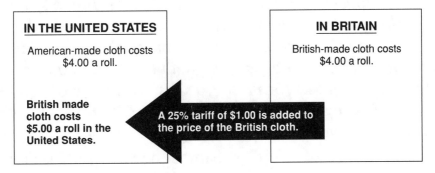

   Which statement correctly identifies the purpose of a tariff in regards to people of the early American nation?

   1. A tariff would allow farmers to sell their crops in Britain.
   2. A tariff helps the government raise money to operate and helps American manufacturers.
   3. A tariff would allow British cloth producers an equal chance to earn profits in the United States.
   4. A tariff allows American manufacturers the opportunity to make their cloth cheaper than their British counterparts.

   4. _____

5. In what area would an archaeologist find evidence of the Aztec civilization?

   1. southwestern United States
   2. Mexico
   3. on the Great Plains
   4. Peru

   5. _____

6. Which of the following was a representative assembly that made local laws for Jamestown?

   1. Mayflower Compact
   2. House of Burgesses
   3. General Court
   4. Virginia Company

   6. _____

7. Read this quotation then answer the question that follows.

   I had much conversation with them (the Huron Indians) regarding the source of the great river and regarding their country, both of the rivers, falls, lakes, and lands and of the tribes living there . . . In short they spoke to me of these things in great detail . . . taking pleasure in telling me about them. And as for myself, I was not weary of listening to them because some things were cleared up about which I had been in doubt until they enlightened me about them.

   Samuel de Champlain, French explorer

   Which statement shows Champlain's attitude toward the Huron Indians?

   1. He believed there was much the white man could teach them.
   2. He felt they would be difficult to defeat in battle.
   3. He hoped that the French and Indians would become trading partners.
   4. He found them useful in providing information to help his exploration.

   7. _____

8. Which action is the best example of checks and balances?
   1. voting in the electoral college
   2. the president vetoing a bill
   3. Congress voting on a new bill
   4. the Supreme Court passing a bill

   8. _____

9. The Three-Fifths Compromise dealt with which of the following issues?
   1. taxation without representation
   2. creation of a two-house legislative body
   3. counting of the slave population for representation
   4. importing slaves into the country

   9. _____

10. The variety of peoples and ideas in the Middle Colonies contributed to
    1. free education for all.
    2. prejudice and a lack of unity.
    3. the spread of slavery.
    4. tolerance and prosperity.

    10. _____

11. The purpose of the Bill of Rights is to
    1. support the federal government.
    2. secure the rights of the president.
    3. support the idea of checks and balances.
    4. protect the basic rights of citizens.

    11. _____

12. Use your knowledge of social studies and the excerpt from Frederick Douglass' writing to answer the question.

    The white man's happiness cannot be purchased by the black man's misery. . . . It is evident that white and black must fall or flourish together . . . laws ought to be enacted . . . and every right and privilege . . . now enjoyed by the white man, ought to be as freely granted to the man of color.

    North Star, 1849

    During the 1800s, Frederick Douglass was a person who wanted
    1. all slaves to be treated fairly.
    2. all whites to purchase a black man's happiness.
    3. whites and blacks to be treated equally.
    4. whites and blacks to enact laws.

    12. _____

13. Using the excerpt from George Washington's Farewell Address and your knowledge of social studies answer the question below.

Observe good faith and justice towards all nations. Cultivate peace and harmony with all . . . It is our true policy to steer clear of permanent alliances, with any portion of the foreign world . . . Taking care always to keep ourselves . . . on a respectively defensive posture, we may safely trust to temporary alliances for extraordinary means . . . The great rule of conduct for us in regard to foreign nations is in extending our commercial relations to have as little political connection as possible . . .

George Washington's Farewell Address, 1796

Which statement correctly identifies George Washington's feelings as he left office?

1. The United States should always help France during a war because France helped the United States achieve independence from Great Britain.
2. The United States is a strong nation that should form military alliances in order to help its economy.
3. The American people should concentrate on building its economy and not form military alliances.
4. The American people should be concerned with building a great nation that requires strong commercial and military connections with other nations.

13. _____

14. Use your knowledge of social studies and the quotation below to answer the question.

A house divided against itself cannot stand . . . I do not expect the Union to be dissolved. I do not expect the house to fall but I do expect it will cease to be divided. It will become all one thing or all the other.

Abraham Lincoln, 1858

What issue is Abraham Lincoln referring to in this quotation?

1. women's rights
2. voting rights for blacks
3. slavery
4. westward expansion

14. _____

15. Use the passage from Abraham Lincoln and your knowledge of social studies to answer the question below.

If I could save the Union without freeing any slave, I would do it; if I could save it by freeing all the slaves, I would do it; and if I could save it by freeing some and leaving others alone, I would also do that.

Abraham Lincoln, 1862

Soon after Lincoln wrote the words above, he issued the

1. Emancipation Proclamation
2. Gettysburg Address
3. Conscription Act
4. Union Plan of Battle

15. _____

16. How did the North and South differ just before the Civil War?

1. The North had more cities and factories than the South.
2. The North was more rural than the South.
3. The North did not have as many immigrants as the South.
4. The Northern laborers were more likely to be African-Americans.

16. _____

17. Use this quotation and your knowledge of social studies to answer the question below.

The laborer has now more comforts than the farmer had a few generations ago. The farmer has more luxuries than the landlord had and is more richly clothed and better housed. The landlord has books and pictures rarer and more artistic than the king had.

Andrew Carnegie

In this statement, Andrew Carnegie claims that the growth of industry has

1. created economic hardships for most people.
2. increased political power of farmers.
3. led to ideal working conditions in factories.
4. improved the way most people live.

17. _____

18. Which statement about reform movements in America is true?

    1. They seek better conditions for people living in rural areas.
    2. They are concentrated in the Midwest and Western states.
    3. They want to improve people's standard of living.
    4. They were a direct result of reform movements taking place in Europe.

    18. _____

19. "Give me liberty or give me death! Since nothing but blows will do, let us come to a final separation!" These statements are the words of

    1. Loyalists
    2. British officials
    3. Redcoats
    4. Patriots

    19. _____

20. In 1906, John Spargo made the following statement:

    Crouched over the (coal) chutes, the boys sit hour after hour, picking out the pieces of slate and other refuse . . . I once stood in a breaker for half an hour and tried to do the work a twelve-year old boy was doing day after day, for ten hours at a stretch, for sixty cents a day. The gloom of the breaker appalled me . . .

    Based on this statement, John Spargo was most likely

    1. a muckraker.
    2. an industrialist.
    3. a factory owner.
    4. an Abolitionist.

    20. _____

21. "Connecticut wants no Massachusetts men in her corps. And Massachusetts thinks there is no necessity for a Rhode Islander to be introduced to her."

    This quotation from General Washington during the Revolutionary War suggests that many of his soldiers

    1. were Loyalists who would not serve with the Continental Army.
    2. felt more loyalty to their home states than to the Continental Army.
    3. were afraid to fight the British.
    4. could not follow orders and maintain discipline.

    21. _____

22. Which of the following statements is true about big business in the late 1800s?

    1. Business leaders encouraged competition.
    2. Large corporations forced many smaller businesses to close.
    3. Investors were unwilling to lend money to corporations.
    4. The government took over many failing businesses.

    22. _____

23. The governing body that ruled the former thirteen colonies during the Revolutionary War was called the

    1. House of Burgesses.
    2. General Court.
    3. Continental Congress.
    4. Parliament.

    23. _____

24. Several European countries helped the American colonies during the Revolutionary War because those European countries

    1. were in competition with England.
    2. supported the thirteen colonies' demand for freedom.
    3. were promised special trading privileges.
    4. were eager to go to war against England.

    24. _____

25. Which of the following was a result of Prohibition?

    1. Bootleggers suffered.
    2. Many Americans broke the law.
    3. Organized crime decreased.
    4. Most federal government employees became corrupt.

    25. _____

26. A major problem for workers building the Panama Canal was

    1. rebellion among the people of Panama.
    2. French interference.
    3. a lack of money.
    4. a high level of disease.

    26. _____

27. Writers and artists of the Harlem Renaissance were most concerned with the

    1. new clothing styles of the 1920s.
    2. experience of blacks in the United States.
    3. effects of the Ku Klux Klan.
    4. uneven prosperity across the United States.

    27. _____

28. The passage of the Thirteenth, Fourteenth, and Fifteenth Amendments to the Constitution was designed to

1. end the Civil War.
2. aid Reconstruction.
3. increase the power of the South.
4. decrease the power of the federal government.

28. _____

29. During World War I, many black Americans migrated to large urban centers because

1. they no longer liked the climate of the South.
2. discrimination did not exist in the North.
3. jobs were available in war-related industries.
4. Congress encouraged blacks to move to the North.

29. _____

30. Which group would most likely support ideas expressed by the Ku Klux Klan?

1. Abolitionists
2. Suffragists
3. Nativists
4. Feminists

30. _____

31. These headlines refer to events during which period?

"PRESIDENT ORDERS AIRLIFT OF SUPPLIES INTO WEST BERLIN"
"TROOPS CLASH WITH COMMUNISTS IN KOREA"
"KENNEDY WARNS KHRUSHCHEV TO REMOVE MISSILES FROM CUBA"

1. The Progressive Era
2. The Roaring Twenties
3. The Great Depression
4. The Cold War

31. _____

32. "An educated citizen is an informed citizen." This statement supports the idea that

    1. education is important in a democracy.
    2. schools should emphasize science and math courses.
    3. more money needs to be spent on social programs.
    4. only educated people can get good jobs.

    32. _____

33. Which of the following is true about compromise, negotiation, and mediation?

    1. They help bring people who disagree together.
    2. They do not help settle disputes.
    3. They are not effective in crisis situations.
    4. They are unconstitutional.

    33. _____

34. The Supreme Court decision in the *Brown* v. *Board of Education* case in 1954 concerned

    1. segregation in public schools.
    2. separation of church and state.
    3. voting rights for African-Americans.
    4. control of interstate commerce.

    34. _____

35. The Nazis in Germany and the Ku Klux Klan in the United States were similar in that both were

    1. against nationalism.
    2. tolerant of racial and ethnic diversity.
    3. willing to take away the human rights of others.
    4. in favor of communist ideology.

    35. _____

36. The right of women to vote, the direct election of senators, and the prohibition of alcohol came about through

    1. amendments to the Constitution.
    2. laws passed by state legislatures.
    3. decisions by the Supreme Court.
    4. acts of Congress.

    36. _____

37. Which of the following democratic goals was reached most recently?

    1. freedom of press and speech
    2. the extension of voting rights to 18 year olds
    3. freedom of religion
    4. the right to a trial by jury

    37. _____

38. The immediate cause of United States entry into World War I was that the United States

    1. had collective security agreements with Western European nations.
    2. felt it necessary to defend the principle of freedom of the seas.
    3. suffered a direct military attack.
    4. was ready to use its superior military and atomic capabilities.

    38. _____

39. The term "Holocaust" is associated with which action?

    1. the detention of Japanese-Americans by the United States
    2. the bombing of Pearl Harbor by the Japanese
    3. nuclear attack on Japanese cities by the Allies
    4. the mass murder of millions of Jews and others by the Nazis

    39. _____

40. Base your answer to the following question on the cartoon below and your knowledge of social studies.

A Good Time for Reflection

The cartoon entitled "A Good Time for Reflection" from the late 1930s encouraged the American public to

1. exercise caution regarding involvement in European conflicts.
2. demand repayment of World War II debts owed by European nations.
3. support countries resisting communist aggression.
4. provide food to Eastern Europe.

40. _____

41. During the age of industrialization in the late nineteenth century, which group favored government regulation of railroads?

1. Native Americans
2. captains of industry
3. farmers
4. southern sharecroppers

41. _____

42. Which part of the Populist platform was adopted as a result of a constitutional amendment?

POPULIST PLATFORM OF 1892
A. GRADUATED INCOME TAX.
B. THE COINAGE OF SILVER BY THE GOVERNMENT.
C. EIGHT-HOUR WORKDAY FOR FACTORY WORKERS.
D. GOVERNMENT OWNERSHIP AND OPERATION OF RAILROADS.

1. A
2. B
3. C
4. D

42. _____

43. What do Upton Sinclair and Ralph Nader have in common? They both were

1. elected to Congress where they fought for political reform.
2. appointed to judgeships where they ruled against corrupt politicians.
3. responsible for the passage of legislation aimed at correcting abuses facing Americans.
4. criticized for supporting the establishment.

43. _____

44. Roosevelt's plan to pack the Supreme Court came about as a result of

1. the Senate's rejection of one of Franklin Roosevelt's nominees to the Court.
2. a request made by the Chief Justice to increase the size of the Court.
3. Congress' refusal to pass legislation providing relief.
4. decisions made by the Supreme Court declaring New Deal legislation unconstitutional.

44. _____

45. Baby boomers are most concerned with which program passed during the New Deal?

1. Social Security
2. Medicare
3. Welfare
4. Environmental regulation

45. _____

PART II: CONSTRUCTED RESPONSE QUESTIONS

Directions (1-15)

For each question write your answer in the space provided. You may use either pen or pencil to write your answers. If you want to change an answer, cross out or erase your original response. You may not know the answers to some of the questions, but do the best you can on each one.

I. Base your answers to questions 1–4 on the chart below and your knowledge of social studies.

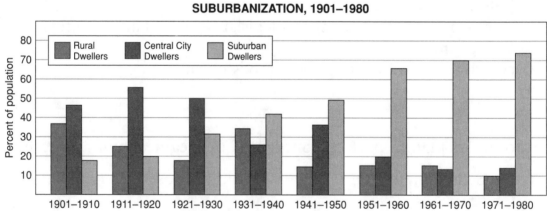

SUBURBANIZATION, 1901–1980

1. What information does this chart present?

_____

_____ (1)

2. During what decade did the greatest number of people live in rural areas?

_____

_____ (1)

3. During what ten-year period did the greatest increase in the number of suburban dwellers occur?

_____

_____ (1)

4. Name two factors that contributed to the change in where people lived from 1951–1980.

_____

_____ (2)

II. Base your answers to questions 5–8 on the 1898 headlines from the front page of *The World* newspaper below and your knowledge of social studies.

5. What incident are the headlines reporting?

_____

_____ (1)

6. What conflict in American history began shortly after this incident?

_____

_____ (1)

7. What kind of journalism did this newspaper practice?

_____

_____ (1)

8. As reflected by this incident, what do we call the type of foreign policy characterized by U.S. involvement in military conflicts for the purposes of gaining overseas territory?

_____

_____ (1)

III. Base your answers to questions 9–12 on the passage below and your knowledge of social studies.

Founding the League of Iroquois

To oppose those hordes of northern tribes, single and alone, would prove certain destruction. We can make no progress in that way. We must unite ourselves into one common band of brothers. We must have but one voice. Many voices make confusion. We must have one fire, one pipe, and one war club. This will give us strength. If our warriors are united, then they can defeat the enemy and drive them from our land; if we do this, we are safe . . . You five great and powerful nations, with your tribes, must unite and have one common interest, and no foe shall disturb or subdue you.

9. What groups of Native Americans does this passage refer to?

   _____

   _____ (1)

10. How many tribes became part of this confederation?

   _____

   _____ (1)

11. Why was it important for the tribes to form the confederation?

   _____

   _____ (1)

12. What were two advantages of the confederation?

   _____

   _____ (1)

IV. Base your answers to questions 13–15 on the map below and your knowledge of social studies.

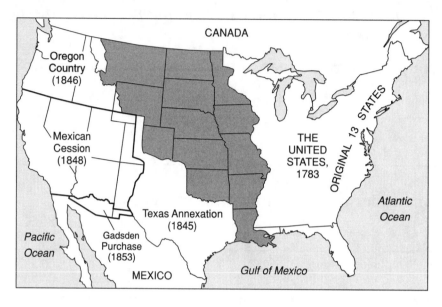

13. How did the United States acquire the shaded area?

_____

_____ (1)

14. Name the last area added to the United States.

_____

_____ (1)

15. Why was this growth of the United States referred to as "Manifest Destiny"?

_____

_____ (2)

PART III: DOCUMENT-BASED QUESTION

Generic Scoring Rubric

5

- ▪ Thoroughly addresses all aspects of the Task by accurately analyzing and interpreting at least four documents
- ▪ Incorporates information from the documents in the body of the essay
- ▪ Incorporates relevant outside information
- ▪ Richly supports the theme or problem with relevant facts, examples, and details
- ▪ Is a well-developed essay, consistently demonstrating a logical and clear plan of organization
- ▪ Introduces the theme or problem by establishing a framework that is beyond a simple restatement of the Task or Historical Context and concludes with a summation of the theme or problem

4

- ▪ Addresses all aspects of the Task by accurately analyzing and interpreting at least four documents
- ▪ Incorporates information from the documents in the body of the essay
- ▪ Incorporates relevant outside information
- ▪ Includes relevant facts, examples, and details, but discussion may be more descriptive than analytical
- ▪ Is a well-developed essay, demonstrating a logical and clear plan of organization
- ▪ Introduces the theme or problem by establishing a framework that is beyond a simple restatement of the Task or Historical Context and concludes with a summation of the theme or problem

3

- ▪ Addresses most aspects of the Task or addresses all aspects of the Task in a limited way, using some of the documents
- ▪ Incorporates some information from the documents in the body of the essay
- ▪ Incorporates limited or no relevant outside information

- Includes some facts, examples, and details, but discussion is more descriptive than analytical
- Is a satisfactorily developed essay, demonstrating a general plan of organization
- Introduces the theme or problem by repeating the Task or Historical Context and concludes by simply repeating the theme or problem

2

- Attempts to address some aspects of the Task, making limited use of the documents
- Presents no relevant outside information
- Includes few facts, examples, and details; discussion restates contents of the documents
- Is a poorly organized essay, lacking focus
- Fails to introduce or summarize the theme or problem

1

- Shows limited understanding of the Task with vague, unclear references to the documents
- Presents no relevant outside information
- Includes little or no accurate or relevant facts, details, or examples
- Attempts to complete the Task, but demonstrates a major weakness in organization
- Fails to introduce or summarize the theme or problem

0

- Fails to address the Task, is illegible, or is a blank

Part III: Document-Based Question

This question is based on the accompanying documents (1–7). Some of the documents have been edited for the purpose of the question. The question is designed to test your ability to work with historical documents. As you analyze the documents take into account both the context of each document and any point of view that may be presented in the document.

Directions: This document-based question consists of two parts. Use black or dark ink to answer the question.

Historical Context

Immigration in the United States has had both positive and negative effects on the immigrant and on life in the United States. The following documents express various points of view about the history of immigration in the United States.

Task

Using information from the documents and your knowledge of social studies, answer the questions that follow each document in Part A. Your answers to the questions will help you write the Part B essay in which you will be asked to:

- ▪ Evaluate both the positive and the negative effects of immigration on the immigrant and on life in the United States.

Part A—Short Answer

Directions: Analyze the documents and answer the questions that follow each document in the space provided. Your answers to questions will help you write the essay.

Document 1: The picture below was taken from Frank Leslie's *Sunday Magazine* of March 1881.

1. The picture portrays these Chinese immigrants engaged in what activity?

   _____

   _____ (1)

2. What effect could this activity have on their lives in the United States?

   _____

   _____ (1)

Document 2: The quote below was taken from an interview with Roland Damani, an immigrant shoe machinery worker in 1938.

The children of Italian immigrants wish most of all to become Americans. They make haste to adopt the American customs and speech. In fact they worry and grieve their parents, who cannot understand or keep pace with them. It is not a little tragic sometimes, this conflict between the children and their elders.

3. What conflict existed between parent and child in the immigrant family?

   _____

   _____ (1)

4. According to Roland Damani, what was one positive and one negative effect on the immigrant family?

   _____

   _____ (2)

Document 3: The following political cartoon appeared in the magazine, *Judge*, in 1903.

5. After looking at this political cartoon list one positive and one negative effect of immigration on life in the United States. (2)

Positive Effect:

_____ (1)

Negative Effect:

_____ (1)

Document 4: The following passage was taken from a speech to Congress in 1908 by Representative Samuel McMillan of New York.

Where would your mines have been dug and worked, where would your great iron industries and constructions . . . have been were it not for the immigrants? . . . It is the immigrant that bears the burden of hard labor . . . and has contributed his full share to the building up of our great country.

6. What were two contributions, according to Representative McMillan, that immigrants have made on life in the United States?

_____

_____ (2)

Document 5: The following quotes were taken from a Polish immigrant and a Vietnamese-Cambodian immigrant.

Everybody lived in little cliques, the Polish, the Ukrainian, the Russian. So they would help each other out, whatever. Maybe one knew a few words more than the other. They used to live, I don't know how many, maybe ten, twelve people in one room because one was helping the other to get established here.

When I was in elementary, I wanted to make friends with the American people. At first I come, I don't speak English, I just want to say "Hi." And then they just walk away. They gave me a look and then what's wrong with that. And then the American people and Spanish people, they start calling me "Chink! Chink!" And after that I know that people don't like each other in America.

7. Identify one problem each person faced as a new immigrant in the United States.

_____

_____ (2)

Document 6: Answer the questions below based upon the cartoon by Thomas Nast, entitled "The Chinese Question" and your knowledge of social studies.

THE CHINESE QUESTION.—
COLUMBIA—"HANDS OFF, GENTLEMEN! AMERICA MEANS FAIR PLAY FOR ALL MEN."

8. What is Nast's point of view on the subject of immigration?

_____

_____ (1)

9. What does the woman in the cartoon mean when she says "Hands off, Gentlemen! America means fair play for all men."

_____

_____ (1)

Document 7: Answer the questions below based upon the two cartoons of the Statue of Liberty, each with differing points of view on immigration, and your knowledge of social studies.

"Give me your tired, your poor, your huddled masses yearning to breathe free, the wretched refuse of your teeming shore. Send these, the homeless, tempest-tost to me, I lift my lamp beside the golden door!"

Emma Lazarus
"The New Colossus," 1883

Passage 1

Give me
your scientists,
your doctors,
your teachers,
but keep your
huddled masses
to yourselves.

Adapted From: *World Press Review,*
November 1980

Passage 2

10. Identify the point of view of each cartoon.

_____ (1)

_____ (1)

11. Which cartoon reflects a positive outlook towards immigration?

_____

_____ (1)

Part B—Essay

Directions:

- Write a well-organized essay that includes an introduction, several paragraphs, and a conclusion.
- Use evidence from the documents to support your response.
- Include specific related outside information.
- Use black or dark ink to write your essay.

Historical Context
Immigration in the United States has had both positive and negative effects on the immigrant and on life in the United States. The documents provided express various points of view about the history of immigration in the United States.

Task

Using information from the documents and your knowledge of social studies, answer the questions that follow each document in Part A. Your answers to the questions will help you write the Part B essay in which you will be asked to:

■ Evaluate both the positive and the negative effects of immigration on the immigrant and on life in the United States.

Be sure to include specific historical details. You must also include additional information from your knowledge of social studies.

_____

_____

_____

_____

_____

_____

_____

_____

_____

_____

_____

MODEL EXAMINATION 1 ANSWERS

Part I: Multiple-Choice Answer Key

Please note that the Roman numeral next to the answer represents the scope and sequence Unit and the Arabic Number represents the Standard. (See chart below).

1.	4	I-2	16.	1	VI-3	31.	4	XI-1
2.	2	II-1	17.	4	VII-4	32.	1	CT-1
3.	3	II-5	18.	3	VII-1	33.	1	CT-1
4.	2	III-4	19.	4	III-1	34.	1	XI-5
5.	2	I-3	20.	1	VII-1	35.	3	CT-1
6.	2	II-5	21.	2	III-1	36.	1	CT-5
7.	4	II-1	22.	2	VII-4	37.	2	XI-5
8.	2	IV-5	23.	3	III-5	38.	2	XI-1
9.	3	III-5	24.	1	III-2	39.	4	XI-2
10.	4	II-1	25.	2	IX-1	40.	1	X-1
11.	4	IV-5	26.	4	VIII-1	41.	3	VII-5
12.	3	V-1	27.	2	IX-1	42.	1	VII-5
13.	3	III-1	28.	2	VI-5	43.	3	CT-5
14.	3	VI-1	29.	3	VIII-3	44.	4	IX-5
15.	1	VI-5	30.	3	IX-1	45.	1	XI-4

GRADE EIGHT INTERMEDIATE SOCIAL STUDIES TEST SPECIFICATIONS GRID
MULTIPLE-CHOICE ITEMS BY STANDARD AND UNIT

↓ Unit / Standard →	1 US and NY History	2 World History	3 Geography	4 Economics	5 Civics, Citizenship, and Government	Number
1–Prior to 1500	0	1	5	0	0	2
2–Exploration/Colonization	2, 7, 10	0	0	0	3, 6	5
3–A Nation Created	13, 19, 21	24	0	4	9, 23	7
4–Experiment in Government	0	0	0	0	8, 11	2
5–Life in a New Nation	12	0	0	0	0	1
6–Division and Reunion	14	0	16	0	15, 28	4
7–An Industrial Society	18, 20	0	0	17, 22	41, 42	6
8–An Interdependent World	26	0	29	0	0	2
9–Between the Wars	25, 27, 30	0	0	0	44	4
10–Worldwide Responsibilities	40	0	0	0	0	1
11–WW II to the Present	31, 38	39	0	45	34, 37	6
11*–Cross-Topical	32, 33, 35	0	0	0	36, 43	5
Total						45

*Items placed in row 11 are cross-topical. Cross-topical items address content from two or more units.

Part I: Multiple-Choice Answers Explained

1. **4** After the first Spanish explorers discovered gold and other riches in the New World, Spain set up colonies for the purpose of protecting its claims to New World territories and their riches. By the middle of the 1500s, Spain had established a large colonial empire in the New World. It included the land around the Mississippi River, Florida, Mexico, Central America, South America, and the Caribbean Islands.

Wrong Choices Explained:

(1) The fur-trading industry was established in Canada and other northern non-Spanish territories.

(2) People from Spain did not want to establish new homes in the New World. Unlike people from England, who fled from that country for religious and political reasons, Spain's settlements were largely created by explorers looking for wealth.

(3) Though Spain engaged in the slave trade, it did not capture them in the New World.

2. **2** Tobacco, indigo, and rice were all important products to the Southern colonies. The Southern colonies grew tobacco and then used it to trade for indigo and rice.

Wrong Choices Explained:

(1) Iron and copper were not produced in large amounts during colonial times.

(3) Fish and lumber were important products to the New England colonies.

(4) Barley, corn, and rye were agricultural products important to the Middle Atlantic colonies.

3. **3** The New York State Constitution provides for a two-house legislature consisting of a State Assembly and a State Senate. The United States Constitution provides for a two-house legislature consisting of the House of Representatives and the Senate.

Wrong Choices Explained:

(1) By definition a federal system of government is a national system of government consisting of a central government and local or state

governments. The New York State Constitution only addresses the state of New York.

(2) The electoral college provides a mechanism for electing the president of the United States.

(4) United States senators are elected every six years. New York State legislators are elected every two years.

4. **2** The definition of a tariff is a tax on imports. Looking at the illustration, you see that the arrow points to an increase of 25 percent on British made cloth entering the United States. Therefore, American cloth that costs $4 a roll would be 25 percent less expensive than the British cloth entering the United States. American cloth manufacturers get the benefit of being able to sell their goods at a lower price than the British manufacturers and the taxes paid by the British raise revenues for the government.

Wrong Choices Explained:

(1) A tariff on British cloth would have no affect on the ability of farmers to sell their goods to Britain. Remember, the definition of a tariff is a tax on imported goods.

(3) If a tariff is imposed on British goods, it will be impossible for British producers to have an equal chance to earn profits because they must pay a 25 percent import tax that American manufacturers do not have to pay.

(4) The effect of a tariff is to increase the price of foreign goods brought into the country. Therefore, domestic manufacturers are able to sell their products at a cheaper price than foreign manufacturers. A tariff, however, does not make it any cheaper for a domestic manufacturer to actually produce its goods.

5. **2** Since the Aztec civilization first developed in Mexico, an archaeologist, a person who studies past lives and cultures using relics from ancient civilizations, would have to look there to find evidence from that civilization.

Wrong Choices Explained:

(1) Relics of Native American civilizations such as the Palute and Ute would be found in the Southwestern United States.

(3) Relics of civilizations such as the Sioux and Cheyenne would be found on the Great Plains.

(4) Relics of the Inca civilization would be found in Peru.

6. **2** Colonists in Jamestown, founded by British settlers in 1607, were allowed to establish a legislature called the House of Burgesses in 1619. Elected representatives could propose the laws that the appointed governor could veto, or refuse to sign. The House of Burgesses was the first representative legislature in the colonies.

Wrong Choices Explained:

(1) The Mayflower Compact was the agreement made by the Pilgrims that created a civil government for the colony they established after landing at Plymouth Rock.

(3) A general court was a court of law that was set up in the colonies.

(4) The Virginia Company was a trading company that operated in the Virginia colony.

7. **4** Samuel de Champlain, hired by France to establish fur-trading ports in Canada, founded the settlement of Quebec in 1608. Quebec eventually became a trading post and a fort. Champlain's conversation with the Huron Indians provided him with a great deal of information about the tribe and the geography of their land. This information helped Champlain with his exploration.

Wrong Choices Explained:

(1) The quotation indicates just the opposite. By listening to the Huron, Champlain indicated that he learned a great deal from them.

(2) Nowhere in the conversation is there any indication that Champlain and the Huron tribe were about to engage in battle.

(3)Though the settlement became a trading post, there is no evidence in the quotation that Champlain hoped to become a trading partner with the Huron.

8. **2** The principle of checks and balances, found in the U.S. Constitution, is extremely important. Through checks and balances, one branch of government can use its power to prevent another branch from becoming too powerful. An example of checks and balances is the veto power of the

president. The president can veto, or prevent, a bill proposed by Congress from becoming a law. In this example, the president, through his veto, checks the power of Congress.

Wrong Choices Explained:

(1) The electoral college does not involve any principle of checks and balances. The electoral college, established by the Constitution, elects the president based on the popular vote of the people and does not impose a limitation on the power of any branch of the federal government.

(3) The power of Congress to vote on a new bill does not represent any principle of checks and balances. As it is the function of Congress to propose laws, its power to do so does not represent a limitation on any other branch of government.

(4) This is an incorrect statement as the Supreme Court does not have the power to pass a bill. The Supreme Court's ability to decide whether a law is constitutional, however, represents a check on the power of Congress to enact laws.

9. **3** The Three-Fifths Compromise, reached during the Constitutional Convention in 1787, established, for purposes of representation in the House of Representatives, that every five slaves would count as three people. The compromise allowed Southern states greater representation in Congress.

Wrong Choices Explained:

(1) Taxation without representation was a grievance of the colonists found in the Declaration of Independence.

(2) Creation of a two-house legislative body, with every state receiving equal representation in the Senate and representation based on population in the House of Representatives, was a result of the Great Compromise.

(4) The importation of slaves, allowed until 1808, was not addressed by the Three-Fifths Compromise.

10. **4** The Middle Colonies included New York (founded in 1624), Massachusetts (founded in 1629), Connecticut (founded in 1633), Maryland (founded in 1634), Rhode Island (founded in 1636), and Delaware (founded in 1638). People who sought to escape religious persecution as well as people who sought to expand trade settled these colonies. This diversity of

early colonists contributed to the tolerance and prosperity of the Middle Colonies.

Wrong Choices Explained:

(1) Though education was available in the Middle Colonies, it was not offered to all the people. For instance, women were excluded.

(2) As many of the colonists in the Middle Colonies came to escape religious persecution, they opposed prejudice and were unified in their belief in tolerance.

(3) Settlers in the Middle Colonies did not favor slavery.

11. **4** The Bill of Rights, the first ten amendments to the Constitution, were added in 1791 to protect the rights of the citizens against the abuses of the federal government. These rights include freedom of speech, freedom of religion, freedom of the press, freedom to assemble and petition the government, the right to bear arms, the right against unreasonable search and seizure as well as due process rights including the right to an attorney, and the right to a fair trial.

Wrong Choices Explained:

(1) The Bill of Rights guarantees certain basic rights that the federal government cannot take away from its citizens. Therefore, the Bill of Rights limits, not supports, the power of the federal government.

(2) Article II of the Constitution, not the Bill of Rights, secures the rights of the president in the executive branch of the federal government.

(3) The principle of checks and balances does not deal with the rights of citizens. It prevents one branch of government from becoming too powerful.

12. **3** Frederick Douglass was a freed slave and an Abolitionist who fought to end slavery. As an editor for an Abolitionist newspaper, Douglass gave speeches around the country. The quotation from the newspaper, *North Star*, urged the passage of laws that would treat both whites and blacks equally.

Wrong Choices Explained:

(1) Though Douglass certainly wanted all slaves to be treated fairly, the quotation deals with Douglass' desire to end slavery. The use of the word *all* should also give you a clue that this cannot be the answer.

(2) The quotation indicates the opposite. Douglass clearly states that blacks and whites should be treated equally through enactment of laws, not by whites purchasing the happiness of slaves. The use of the word *all* should also give you a clue that this cannot be the answer.

(4) While the quotation indicates that Douglass wanted laws passed that would treat blacks and whites equally, he does not say that he wants whites and blacks to enact laws together. In fact, it was impossible for blacks, at that time, to enact laws because they had no rights.

13. **3** Washington delivered his Farewell Address when he left office. It urged future leaders not to form permanent alliances and to remain neutral in world affairs, and it became the foundation of American foreign policy throughout most of the nineteenth century. The passage clearly indicates Washington's two desires, for the United States to build up its commercial relations with other countries and for the country to stand clear of political alliances.

Wrong Choices Explained:
(1) This statement is clearly wrong for two reasons. First, there is no mention of France anywhere in the passage. Second, the passage clearly indicates Washington's desire for the country to stand clear of any political alliances with foreign countries.

(2) This statement is incorrect because at the time of Washington's Farewell Address the United States was still in its infancy, and not a strong nation. Washington believed that America should concentrate on developing its economy through commercial relations.

(4) The statement is misleading. Washington wanted the country to remain neutral so that it could develop into a great nation. However, he felt that military connections with other nations would prevent that goal.

14. **3** Lincoln delivered this speech prior to his inauguration as president and it is one of the most famous speeches he ever made. In the speech, Lincoln talks about "a house divided," referring to the division between the North and South over the issue of slavery. The speech also states Lincoln's belief that he does "not expect the Union to be dissolved." This clearly refers to the Southern states' threat to secede from the Union upon Lincoln's inauguration because they believed he would abolish slavery.

Wrong Choices Explained:

(1) Lincoln was not addressing the issue of women's rights in this speech.

(2) Lincoln was not addressing the issue of voting rights for blacks. That issue was resolved after the Civil War with the passage of the Fifteenth Amendment in 1870.

(4) While westward expansion was a factor in the debate over slavery, Lincoln was not addressing that issue in the speech.

15. **1** Soon after writing those words, Lincoln issued the Emancipation Proclamation in 1862, which freed the slaves only in the Confederacy. Lincoln felt that if he issued an order freeing slaves in all of the states, he would lose the support of the border states of the Union that still had slavery.

Wrong Choices Explained:

(2) Lincoln's Gettysburg Address was delivered after the Battle of Gettysburg in 1863. This was one of the bloodiest battles of the Civil War and Lincoln used the occasion to make a statement that he hoped would send a message of healing to the nation.

(3) The Conscription Act was passed during the Civil War for the purpose of instituting a military draft.

(4) The Union Plan of Battle was the strategy established by the Union army during the Civil War.

16. **1** The sectional differences that existed in the United States prior to the Civil War were major factors in the war itself. Political, economic, and social differences were evident between the North and the South. One of the most significant differences between the two was the number of big cities like New York and Philadelphia in the North and its industrial economy and many factories. The South's economy was characterized by a plantation system with its reliance on slavery.

Wrong Choices Explained:

(2) The North was more urban, not more rural, than the South.

(3) The North did have more immigrants than the South. Immigrants settled in Northern cities to work in factories.

(4) Southern laborers, mostly slaves, were more likely to be African-Americans. Northern laborers were more likely to be non-black immigrants who settled in the big cities to work in factories.

17. **4** Andrew Carnegie was known as a "Captain of Industry." He created a monopoly in the steel industry and became the richest man in America. After Carnegie retired, he became a philanthropist, donating large sums of money to charity. Carnegie Hall in New York City is named after him. As an industrialist, the quote indicates Carnegie's belief that industrial growth resulted in an increased standard of living and an improved way of life for most Americans.

Wrong Choices Explained:

(1) While the growth of industry did create economic hardships for some, the passage clearly indicates Carnegie's belief that rapid industrialization benefited the vast majority of Americans.

(2) While American farmers did increase their political power through movements like the Grangers, the quote does not imply that Carnegie believed that industrialization was responsible for that increased power.

(3) While the passage indicates Carnegie's belief that industrialization improved living conditions, it does not imply that he believed industrial growth created ideal working conditions in factories. Long hours, dangerous working conditions, poor pay, and child labor were all by-products of industrialization.

18. **3** The history of reform movements in America revolve around an effort on the part of the reformers to improve people's quality of life. Whether it was an Abolitionist, who wanted to abolish slavery, or a muckraker, who wanted to improve the conditions in factories, reformers had a common goal—to improve the standard of living for Americans.

Wrong Choices Explained:

(1) Reform movements throughout American history have sought better conditions for people living in rural areas as well as people living in cities.

(2) Early reform movements were concentrated in the big cities of the Northeast, not in the Midwest and Western states.

(4) American reform movements were not a result of similar movements taking place in Europe. In fact, European reform movements often lagged behind those of America because there were fewer democratic governments in Europe.

19. **4** Patrick Henry made this statement at the beginning of the American Revolution. As an American patriot, Henry wanted liberty from England and sought to defeat Great Britain in the American Revolution. The "final separation" refers to the American colonies' independence from England.

Wrong Choices Explained:
(1) This statement would not have been made by Loyalists, colonists loyal to England during the American Revolution, because they did not want a "final separation" from England.
(2) This statement would not have been made by British officials because they did not want the American colonies to gain their independence.
(3) This statement would not have been made by Redcoats, British soldiers fighting against the American colonists, because they did not want the American colonies to gain their independence.

20. **1** Muckrakers were Progressive Era authors who investigated and wrote about the problems facing the country, including terrible working conditions, in books, newspapers, and magazines. Spargo's description highlights the terrible conditions encountered by coal miners, and makes it obvious that he was one of the muckrakers who exposed the abuses of the coal mining industry.

Wrong Choices Explained:
(2) Spargo would not have made this statement if he had been an industrialist, a person who invests in big businesses and factories. Most of the terrible working conditions encountered during the Progressive Era were a result of industrialists' greed.
(3) Spargo would not have made this statement if he had been a factory owner. The poor conditions encountered by early factory workers were the result of factory owners' greed.
(4) Spargo would not have made this statement if he had been Abolitionist. Abolitionists were concerned with ending slavery, not improving the working conditions of coal miners.

21. **2** Washington's quote reflects the fact that colonial soldiers were more loyal to their individual home states than to the Continental Army. Remember, the original thirteen colonies all developed with their own dis-

tinctive characteristics, and therefore, soldiers felt more allegiance to the colony where they came from than to the new country.

Wrong Choices Explained:

(1) Loyalists were colonists who remained loyal to the British, and therefore, would not have served in Washington's Continental Army.

(3) The quote does not indicate that Washington believed that his troops were afraid of fighting the British.

(4) Washington's quote does not suggest that his soldiers could not follow orders or maintain discipline.

22. **2** The period of the late 1800s was known as the "Gilded Age." It was characterized by the growth of big business and a policy of *laissez-faire* (hands-off) by the government. Industrialists like Carnegie and Rockefeller formed large corporations and used their power to create monopolies. These monopolies reduced and, in many cases, eliminated competition from smaller businesses.

Wrong Choices Explained:

(1) Business leaders during the late 1800s discouraged competition through monopolies and trusts.

(3) Investors were willing to lend money to corporations during the big business boom of the late 1800s. In return, the investors received stock in the business they invested in.

(4) During the late 1800s, the government pursued a *laissez-faire* policy towards business, allowing corporations to act free of governmental regulations. The government would not have taken over failing business because to do so would violate that policy.

23. **3** The First Continental Congress was formed in 1774 and consisted of representatives from the thirteen colonies. Members passed different resolutions designed to let Great Britain know that the colonists were unhappy with British policies towards the colonies. The Second Continental Congress was responsible for drafting and passing the Declaration of Independence, and it remained the governing body of the colonies even after the Revolutionary War. The Second Continental Congress approved the Articles of Confederation.

Wrong Choices Explained:

(1) The House of Burgesses was the legislative body of the Virginia colony and the first representative legislature in the American colonies.

(2) The General Court was a British court of law established in the colonies.

(4) Parliament is the governing body of Great Britain.

24. **1** As England was the dominant European power with a worldwide empire, other European nations aided the colonies during the Revolutionary War because they were in competition with England for colonial territories in the New World and wanted to see England defeated. These countries had lost out to England in their quest for territorial gains in America. One European country that aided the American colonies was France, which entered the war in 1778. The French General, Lafayette, came to America at his own expense. The entry of France into the war was a significant factor in the victory against the British.

Wrong Choices Explained:

(2) While other European nations aided the colonists, they were more interested in hurting England than in helping the colonists win their freedom.

(3) The European nations that helped the colonists were not promised anything in return for their assistance.

(4) The other European countries that helped the colonists sought to weaken England's power in the New World. However, they did not want a direct war with England, which was the most powerful country in the world at that time.

25. **2** Prohibition, enacted by the Eighteenth Amendment in 1919, made the production, distribution, and sale of alcohol illegal. However, many Americans believed that the government had no right to legislate morality—the consumption of alcohol—and ignored the ban. People made alcohol in their bathtubs, and illegal bars called "speakeasies" sprang up around the country. In 1933, the Twenty-first Amendment was enacted to repeal the Eighteenth Amendment and alcohol was again legal.

Wrong Choices Explained:

(1) Bootleggers, those people who illegally made and sold alcohol, prospered during Prohibition.

(3) During Prohibition, the activities of organized crime increased. Gangsters like Al Capone got rich through the illegal distribution of alcohol.

(4) While Prohibition did cause corruption among government employees, most corruption occurred at the state level.

26. **4** A major problem for workers building the Panama Canal was the high level of disease. Many of those working on the canal became seriously ill and died from Yellow Fever (malaria), an infectious disease spread by mosquitoes.

Wrong Choices Explained:

(1) The people of Panama rebelled against Colombia in 1903, before the start of construction.

(2) There was no French interference as France gave the rights to build the canal to the United States when the French company originally hired went out of business.

(3) Workers were not hampered by a lack of money as the United States funded the building of the canal.

27. **2** The Harlem Renaissance, which took place in Harlem, New York, after World War I, was noted for the expression of the black experience in America by writers, musicians, and other artists. Also called the "Black Renaissance" (rebirth) and the "New Negro Movement" this rebirth of black culture included artists such as Langston Hughes, James Weldon Johnson, and Countee Cullen. Throughout this period, Harlem was the intellectual and cultural center for black Americans.

Wrong Choices Explained:

(1) The new clothing styles of the Roaring Twenties, most notably that of the "Flappers," were not part of the Harlem Renaissance.

(3) While the Harlem Renaissance explored the black experience in America, it did not address the effects of the Ku Klux Klan.

(4) The issue of uneven prosperity across the United States was not one of the concerns of the writers and artists of the Harlem Renaissance.

28. **2** The Thirteenth, Fourteenth, and Fifteenth Amendments, known as the Civil War Amendments, were enacted as part of Reconstruction, following the end of the Civil War. Their purpose was to aid in the re-admittance

of the Confederate states into the Union. The Thirteenth Amendment, passed in 1865, prohibited slavery. The Fourteenth Amendment, passed in 1868, gave freed slaves citizenship rights and equal protection under the law. The Fifteenth Amendment, passed in 1870, gave freed slaves the right to vote. These three amendments had to be accepted by the defeated Southern states as part of the Reconstruction plan enacted by Congress before they could reenter the Union.

Wrong Choices Explained:

(1) The amendments, adopted after the Civil War, were not designed to end the conflict.

(3) The purpose of the amendments was to decrease the power of the Southern states to discriminate against former slaves. By requiring the South to adopt the amendments, the federal government hoped that former slaves would be guaranteed equal rights, however, "Jim Crow laws" and other laws were enacted by many Southern states that continued to discriminate against blacks.

(4) The intent of the amendments was to increase the power of the federal government over the defeated Southern states with respect to the way they treated the freed slaves.

29. **3** The early twentieth century was marked by a general migration of black Americans to the big cities of the North, where blacks had the opportunity to work in the factories that had become part of the cities' landscapes. During World War I, the need for war-related materials increased the demand for workers and many black Americans moved North to meet that demand.

Wrong Choices Explained:

(1) The availability of jobs in Northern factories producing war-related materials, not the Southern climate, was the cause of the black migration North during World War I.

(2) Even though there were increased employment opportunities available to black Americans in the North, there was still discrimination against blacks in many Northern states.

(4) Congress did not pass any legislation to motivate black migration to the North.

30. **3** Nativists, people living in the United States who oppose immigration and disliked ethnic, racial, and religious minority groups, would most likely support ideas expressed by the Ku Klux Klan, another group opposed to minority groups.

Wrong Choices Explained:
(1) Abolitionists, people who wanted to abolish slavery, would not be likely to support ideas expressed by the Ku Klux Klan.
(2) Suffragists, people who sought the woman's right to vote, would not be likely to support the ideas expressed by the Ku Klux Klan.
(4) Feminists, activists who wanted more rights for women, would not be likely to support the ideas expressed by the Ku Klux Klan.

31. **4** The headlines refer to events during the Cold War. Beginning in 1945, after the end of World War II, the Cold War was marked by a series of conflicts between the United States and its Western allies, and the Soviet Union. These conflicts included the Berlin airlift, the Korean War, and the Cuban missile crisis.

Wrong Choices Explained:
(1) The Progressive Era, 1898–1916, was characterized by a period of domestic reform.
(2) The Roaring Twenties, 1920–1929, was characterized by a period of economic prosperity and the rise of the American middle class.
(3) The Great Depression, 1929–1941, was characterized by a period of economic collapse and New Deal legislation, initiated by Franklin Roosevelt.

32. **1** This statement supports the idea that education is one of the foundations of a democratic society. During the late twentieth century, education in the United States has been a priority of both the federal and state governments. This concern reflects the belief that an educated person will be an active and informed participant in the political process.

Wrong Choices Explained:
(2) Though many educators believe that science and math courses should be emphasized, the statement best reflects the idea that education is vital to the active participation of citizens in our democracy.

(3) The statement does not support the idea that more money needs to be spent on social programs.

(4) The statement does not support the idea that only educated people can get good jobs. The use of the absolute "only" should give you a hint that this is a wrong choice.

33. **1** Compromise, negotiation, and mediation are all ways of helping people with differences come to an agreement. All three are methods of dispute settlement that have been used to resolve labor disputes as well as disputes among nations.

Wrong Choices Explained:

(2) Compromise, negotiation, and mediation are dispute settlements techniques, and have helped to settle disputes.

(3) Compromise, negotiation, and mediation are effective means of settling disputes and have been used successfully to resolve crisis situations.

(4) There is nothing in the Constitution preventing use of these dispute settlement techniques.

34. **1** The Supreme Court decision in *Brown* v. *Board of Education* (1954) is one of the most important and famous rulings in American history. In the unanimous 9-0 ruling, the Supreme Court declared that segregation in public schools was illegal and stated that "separate but equal was inherently unequal." As a result, public schools across the country began the process of desegregation.

Wrong Choices Explained:

(2) The Supreme Court decision in *Brown* concerned the issue of racial segregation, not the First Amendment issue of separation of church and state.

(3) Voting rights for African-Americans was not at issue in the *Brown* decision.

(4) Interstate commerce was not at issue in the *Brown* case.

35. **3** Both the Nazis and Ku Klux Klan are examples of racist groups that violently deprived racial, ethnic, and religious minorities of their human rights. The Nazis persecuted and murdered over six million Jews and other minorities during the Holocaust. Formed after the Civil War, the Klan

intimidated freed slaves from exercising their rights of citizenship, often by means of violence, including lynching.

Wrong Choices Explained:

(1) The Nazis and Ku Klux Klan were supporters of nationalism and attracted members by claiming that they were trying to preserve national "purity."

(2) Both of these groups were intolerant of other races and groups with different ethnic backgrounds or religious beliefs.

(4) The Nazis and Klan opposed communism.

36. **1** Women's right to vote, the direct election of senators, and the prohibition of alcohol were all the result of amendments to the Constitution. The Nineteenth Amendment (1920) gave the right of women to vote; the Seventeenth Amendment (1913) provided for the direct election of senators; and the Eighteenth Amendment (1919) prohibited the manufacture, sale, and distribution of alcohol in the United States. It was later repealed by the Twenty-first Amendment (1933).

Wrong Choices Explained:

(2) As the women's right to vote, the direct election of senators, and the prohibition of alcohol affected the entire country, it would be impossible for laws passed by an individual state to bring about such nationally significant changes.

(3) Supreme Court decisions interpret existing laws; they do not enact new ones.

(4) These changes were the result of amendments to the Constitution, not acts of Congress.

37. **2** The extension of voting rights to 18 year olds was granted in 1971 by the Twenty-sixth Amendment.

Wrong Choices Explained:

(1) Freedom of the press and speech were guaranteed in 1791 as part of the Bill of Rights.

(3) Freedom of religion was guaranteed in 1791 as part of the Bill of Rights.

(4) The right to a trial by jury was guaranteed in 1791 as part of the Bill of Rights.

38. **2** While World War I began in Europe, in 1914, after the assassination of Archduke Ferdinand in the Balkans, the United States remained neutral until 1917. As part of its policy of unrestricted submarine warfare, Germany sank the *Lusitania* (1915) and then the *Sussex* (1916). To defend the principle of freedom of the seas, President Wilson broke off diplomatic relations and, shortly thereafter, Congress declared war.

Wrong Choices Explained:
(1) The United States did not have any collective security agreements with Western Europe until after World War II, when it formed the North Atlantic Treaty Organization (NATO).
(3) The United States did not suffer a direct military attack until Japan bombed Pearl Harbor in 1941.
(4) The United States was not a superior military power nor did it have atomic capabilities at that time.

39. **4** The term "Holocaust" is associated with the systematic extermination of millions of Jews and other minorities by the Nazis during World War II.

Wrong Choices Explained:
(1) The term "Holocaust" is not associated with American detention of Japanese-Americans during World War II.
(2) The term "Holocaust" is not associated with Japan's sneak attack on Pearl Harbor in 1941.
(3) The term "Holocaust" is not associated with the United States' nuclear attack on two Japanese cities during World War II.

40. **1** The cartoon encouraged the American people to exercise caution regarding involvement in potential European conflicts and to urge U.S. neutrality during the 1930s. The cartoonist draws attention to the problems caused by U.S. involvement in World War I, including American casualties, unpaid war debts, and economic collapse, in order to encourage the American people to urge U.S. neutrality in the impending European conflict.

Wrong Choices Explained:

(2) The cartoon does not encourage Americans to demand repayment of World War II debts. As the United States did not enter World War II until 1941, this could not be at issue during the late 1930s. Although the cartoon mentions unpaid war debts, it is addressing the debts from World War I, the only world war the United States and the world had been involved in at the time of the cartoon.

(3) The cartoon does not encourage Americans to support countries resisting communist aggression. This issue is not addressed in the cartoon at all.

(4) The cartoon does not encourage Americans to provide food for Eastern Europe. This issue is not addressed in the cartoon at all.

41. 3 During the late nineteenth century, farmers favored government regulation of the railroads because as the railroad companies began to fix hauling prices, they created higher shipping costs for farmers. By the late 1800s, farmers in the Midwest formed a society called the Grangers. Its main objective was to push for greater government regulation of the railroads. Many states passed laws restricting the ability of railroads to fix prices.

Wrong Choices Explained:

(1) While Native Americans were thrown off their land and forced to move to reservations in order to make way for the railroads' westward expansion, they did not seek government regulation of the railroads.

(2) Captains of industry, the major industrialists of the time, opposed government regulation of any kind.

(4) Southern sharecroppers did not rely on the railroads and, therefore, did not favor government regulation of the railroads.

42. 1 The graduated income tax, part of the Populist Party platform, was adopted as the result of the Sixteenth Amendment in 1913. The Populist Party emerged in the late 1800s, in response to the Granger movement. This political party developed a philosophy that favored social, political, and economic reform by the federal government. Though the party never succeeded in electing any of its candidates to national office, many of their programs were later passed into law.

Wrong Choices Explained:

(2) The coinage of silver was an economic reform that was never adopted by the government.

(3) The eight-hour workday, though adopted into law by many states during the 1900s, was not the result of a constitutional amendment.

(4) The government did not attempt to regulate the railroads through governmental ownership or operation.

43. 3 Upton Sinclair and Ralph Nader were both responsible for enactment of legislation aimed at correcting abuses faced by Americans. Upton Sinclair was an author during the Progressive Era who wrote *The Jungle* in 1906. As a result, the Pure Food and Drug Act was passed and signed into law. Ralph Nader, a modern day muckraker, led an investigation in the 1970s that led to mandatory seat belts in automobiles.

Wrong Choices Explained:

(1) Neither Sinclair nor Nader were elected to Congress. Nader did run for the presidency in 1996 and 2000 as a candidate for the environmental Green Party.

(2) Neither man was appointed as a judge.

(4) Neither man was criticized for supporting the establishment. Both were applauded for criticizing the government's failure to act to protect the American people.

44. 4 Franklin Roosevelt's plan to "pack" the Supreme Court was the result of Supreme Court decisions declaring parts of his New Deal legislation unconstitutional. As a result, he wanted to increase the size of the Supreme Court in order to appoint six new justices more sympathetic to his causes. Congress did not approve his plan.

Wrong Choices Explained:

(1) Roosevelt's plan was not the result of a Senate rejection of any of Roosevelt's Supreme Court appointments.

(2) Roosevelt's plan was not made at the request of the Chief Justice of the Supreme Court.

(3) Roosevelt's plan was not the result of Congress' refusal to pass legislation providing relief. Congress did pass the New Deal legislation that Roosevelt wanted.

45. 1 Baby boomers, people who were born after the end of World War II and are now facing retirement, are most concerned with Social Security. By 2010, most baby boomers will be eligible for Social Security benefits, passed as part of the New Deal and guaranteeing income to retirees.

Wrong Choices Explained:

(2) Medicare, passed as part of Lyndon Johnson's Great Society legislation, guarantees senior citizens health insurance. It was not part of the New Deal.

(3) Welfare was also a program that was originally passed as part of Great Society legislation and later reformed during the Clinton administration. It provides economic assistance to the unemployed. While of concern to many Americans, the welfare system was not part of the New Deal.

(4) Environmental regulation, although an important issue, was not part of New Deal legislation.

Part II: Constructed Response Scoring Guidelines and Answers Explained

Each item consists of a single prompt or stimulus (a graph, chart, map, timeline, reading passage, etc.) on which two or more open-ended questions are based. In this model exam there are four constructed response items. Each item has three or more questions based on it for a total of 15 questions. In general, short-answer, open-ended questions within a constructed response item are awarded credit in one of two ways. The amount of credit allocated for an individual constructed response question is determined by whether or not the item has a clear-cut answer.

One point is allocated for an individual question that has a clearly defined response and no partially correct response. The correct response is worth one credit and an incorrect response receives zero credit.

Two points are allocated when a question may elicit either a correct response (worth two credits), a partially correct response (worth one credit), or an incorrect response (worth zero credits).

To receive full credit for a response to a constructed response question, you do not have to develop your answer in a complete sentence or sentences. In addition, a **correct** response copied directly from a passage or paraphrased from a passage should also receive full credit.

1. (1 point) The chart presents information dealing with the growth of the suburbs from 1901 to 1980.

Answer Explained:
The chart's title, "Suburbanization, 1901–1980," tells you that the information presented shows the growth in the number of people living in the suburbs by comparing the percentages of people living in rural areas, central cities, and the suburbs broken down for the decades between 1901 and 1980.

2. (1 point) The greatest number of people lived in rural areas during the decade between 1901–1910.

Answer Explained:
By looking at the chart, you should notice that the decade with the largest percentage of rural dwellers, almost 40 percent of the population, was the decade between 1901 and 1910.

3. (1 point) The decade in which the greatest increase in the number of suburban dwellers occurred was 1951–1960.

Answer Explained:
By comparing the percentages of the population living in suburbs for all decades, you should see that the greatest increase in the suburban population took place in the decade between 1951 and 1960, when the percentage of suburban dwellers grew to 65 percent of the population, an increase of almost 16 percent from the previous decade. That is the largest increase in the number of suburban dwellers shown on the chart.

4. (1–2 points) Two factors that contributed to the change in where people lived from 1951–1980 include the movement of families to the suburbs after the "baby boom" that followed World War II and improvements in transportation.

Answer Explained:
Although you know that the chart deals with the growth of the suburbs, you must use your knowledge of social studies and information not provided by the chart to state two reasons why the number of people living in

the suburbs grew between 1951 and 1980. One reason for the rapid growth of the suburbs during this time period was the large movement of people to the suburbs after World War II. In the 1950s, the United States experienced a "baby boom" as returning soldiers started families. These families moved from the cities to the suburbs. Suburbs like Levittown on Long Island attracted many young families. A second reason why the number of people living in the suburbs increased was the improvement in transportation systems, including the growth of the interstate highway system and mass transit, and increased car ownership, which made it easy for people to live in the suburbs and work in city areas.

5. (1 point) The headlines are reporting the sinking of the *U.S.S. Maine.*

Answer Explained:
By reading the newspaper's headlines, you can clearly see that it is reporting the sinking of the U.S. battleship *Maine* in Havana Harbor.

6. (1 point) The Spanish-American War started shortly after this incident.

Answer Explained:
To answer this question, you must rely on your knowledge of social studies. Remember, after the sinking of the *Maine* was reported, the cry, "Remember the *Maine*" was heard throughout the United States. Americans demanded war with Spain to avenge the sinking, which many newspapers claimed to be the result of a Spanish mine. Though Spain denied any responsibility for the incident, the public and Congress pressured President McKinley to declare War. The Spanish-American War began in 1898.

7. (1 point) The type of journalism practiced by this newspaper was called "yellow journalism."

Answer Explained:
Again, you must rely on your knowledge of social studies to answer this question. The emotional and slanted manner in which the headlines describe the sinking of the *Maine* is meant to sensationalize the story for the purpose of selling newspapers. This type of journalism, called "yellow journalism," was common among newspapers of the time, and practiced by publishers like William Randolph Hearst.

8. (1 point) The type of foreign policy reflected by the Spanish-American War and marked by U.S. involvement in military conflicts for the purpose of gaining overseas territory is called imperialism.

Answer Explained:
Imperialism is a type of foreign policy pursued by a country for the purposes of gaining foreign land or colonies. America pursued this policy through the Spanish-American War. As a result, the United States acquired the Philippines, Puerto Rico, and Cuba.

9. (1 point) The Native Americans referred to in this passage are the Iroquois.

Answer Explained:
The title of the passage, "Founding the League of Iroquois," is a clear indicator that it deals with the founding of the League of Iroquois in 1570, a confederation of the Iroquois tribe of Native Americans.

10. (1 point) Five tribes became part of this confederation.

Answer Explained:
The last sentence clearly refers to five "great and powerful nations." These were the Cayuga, Onondaga, Oneida, Seneca, and Mohawk nations.

11. (1 point) It was important for these tribes to unite because by doing so they would be better able to protect their interests.

Answer Explained:
As you read the passage, you should notice how the theme of unity and its advantages are stressed. Unity, through the creation of a confederation of tribes, would allow the Iroquois nations to better protect their interests because a confederation would possess greater military strength than that of the individual tribes.

12. (1–2 points) Two advantages resulting from a confederation of tribes include the ability of the tribes to speak with a united voice and the ability to more easily defeat their enemies through greater military strength.

Answer Explained:
By reading the passage, you should realize that unification of the tribes into the League of Iroquois would allow the tribes to present a united and common voice, rather than those of five individual tribes, when dealing with issues of common interest. Another advantage of the confederation would be the ability to better protect themselves against their enemies. A unified league of tribes would have a larger number of warriors fighting for a common cause than any of the five individual tribes alone would have.

13. (1 point) The United States acquired the area by purchasing it from France in the Louisiana Purchase.

Answer Explained:
By looking at the area on the map, you should know that the land in question was acquired in the Louisiana Purchase. In 1803, President Thomas Jefferson negotiated an agreement with France whereby the United States purchased French land west of the Mississippi River for $15 million. The Louisiana Purchase more than doubled the size of the United States.

14. (1 point) The last area added to the United States is the area on the map marked "Gadsden Purchase."

Answer Explained:
To answer this question, you should be looking for the latest date that territory was added to the United States. The area indicated as the "Gadsden Purchase," purchased in 1853, was the last territory added to the United States according to this map.

15. (1–2 points) The term "Manifest Destiny" was used to describe the growth of the United States because it was commonly believed that it was God's will for the United States to expand its borders from the East Coast to the West Coast.

Answer Explained:
The term "Manifest Destiny," first used in 1845, describes the policy followed by American presidents to increase the territory of the United States during the 1880s and 1890s. During this time, it was believed that God wanted the United States to expand its borders to the Pacific Ocean.

Part III: Document-Based Question—Short Answers Explained

1. (1 point) The illustration shows Chinese immigrants learning English.

Answer Explained:
The illustration depicts Chinese immigrants being taught English by a teacher using a board with pictures of common objects.

2. (1 point) By learning English, Chinese immigrants would be better able to assimilate, or become part of the American culture. Assimilation would make it easier for the Chinese to contribute to American culture and help them gain acceptance.

Answer Explained:
The ability to speak English is one of the most important keys to assimilation into American society. By being able to speak the language, Chinese immigrants would be able to communicate with the rest of the public.

3. (1 point) The quick manner in which the children of Italian immigrants adapted to life in America, by adopting American customs and speech, created conflict between the children of Italian immigrants and their parents.

Answer Explained:
According to the passage, the children of Italian immigrants adapted quickly to life in America, adopting its customs and speech. This concerned their parents because they feared that their children would forget the customs and traditions of their Italian heritage.

4. (1–2 points: 1 point for a positive effect and 1 point for a negative effect) According to the author of the passage, one positive effect on the immigrant family was the fact that children adapted quickly to the ways of America and were better able to assimilate into American culture. One negative effect was that the rapid assimilation into American culture caused conflicts between children and their parents.

Answer Explained:
As the passage clearly indicates, the rapid adoption of the American way of life by children of Italian immigrants had both positive and negative effects.

The fact that the children quickly took up the customs and speech of America made their assimilation into American culture easier. However, this also had a negative effect because parents feared that their children would lose interest in the customs and traditions of their Italian heritage.

5. (1–2 points: 1 point for a positive effect and 1 point for a negative effect) One positive effect of immigration on life in the United States was that immigrants provided a source of cheap labor. One negative effect of immigration on life in the United States was that many immigrants were infected with disease when they arrived in the United States and brought the threat of large outbreaks of illness.

Answer Explained:
In order to list one positive and one negative effect of immigration on life in the United States, look closely at the different characters in the cartoon and what each is saying. One character says that the immigrant gives him cheap labor. The character of "Uncle Sam" also indicates that immigrants provide a good source of labor by stating that immigrants are "muscle" for his country. You can also list a negative effect in the same way. The cartoon shows a man holding a needle who says the immigrant brings sickness, while another character claims that the immigrant is a menace.

6. (1–2 points: 1 point for each contribution) According to the passage, Representative McMillan believes that immigrants contributed to both the mining and iron industries of the United States.

Answer Explained:
The passage, taken from Representative McMillan's speech, clearly indicates the positive impact that immigrants had on the American economy. McMillan states that the hard labor of immigrants has contributed to the development of America's great mining and iron industries.

7. (1–2 points: 1 point for identification of one problem faced by each person) One problem faced by the Polish immigrant was the difficult living conditions that he had to endure, with many families sharing a single room. One problem that the Vietnamese-Cambodian immigrant faced was his inability to speak English.

Answer Explained:
By reading each quote, you should be able to quickly identify one problem mentioned by each immigrant. The Polish immigrant's quote clearly describes that one problem he faced was the crowded living conditions. The quote of the Vietnamese-Cambodian immigrant also describes the problem he faced, the language barriers caused by his inability to speak English.

8. (1 point) The cartoonist has a very sympathetic point of view on the subject of immigration.

Answer Explained:
Thomas Nast, a well-known political cartoonist, shows a sympathetic point of view towards immigration. By looking at the cartoon, entitled "The Chinese Question," you can see that Nast portrays Columbia, the symbol of America, as the protector of the Chinese immigrant who is being threatened by a mob. She tells the mob of people who are opposed to immigration, known as nativists, "Hands off." Through this cartoon, Nast indicates his sympathetic point of view towards immigration by illustrating that America is a land of opportunity for all people.

9. (1 point) Columbia is saying that America is a land of opportunity open to all people.

Answer Explained:
Columbia's statement, "Hands off, gentlemen! America means fair play for all men," signifies the belief that America has always offered all people a better home and a better way of life. Her statement reiterates the belief that immigrants from around the world have always been welcomed and have had the same opportunities and chance for success as everyone else.

10. (1–2 points: 1 point for each cartoon's point of view) Cartoon 1's point of view believes that immigrants should be welcomed to America and expresses a belief that all people, no matter where they come from or what they do, should be given the opportunity to live in America. Cartoon 2's point of view believes in a policy of restricted immigration.

Answer Explained:

Cartoon 1 is based on the famous poem written by Emma Lazarus called the "New Colossus." Written in 1883 as a tribute to the Statue of Liberty, it embraced the idea of open immigration. Cartoon 1 summarizes this idea of open immigration, stating that all immigrants, no matter what their condition, should be welcome in America. Cartoon 2's point of view expresses a belief in restricted immigration by limiting the types of immigrants that should be allowed into the United States. It states that only people like scientists, doctors, and teachers can make contributions to the United States, and, therefore, they should be the only types of immigrants who should be allowed to enter.

11. (1 point) Cartoon 1 reflects a positive outlook towards immigration.

Answer Explained:

Once you understand the point of view of each cartoon, it should be clear that Cartoon 1 has a positive outlook towards immigration by welcoming all immigrants and favoring a policy of open immigration. Cartoon 2 does not reflect a positive outlook because it seeks to restrict immigration by limiting entry to only those people believed to be able to contribute something to American society.

Part III: Document-Based Question—Sample Student Response Essay

Based on the Specific Scoring Rubric, beginning on page 199, the sample student response essay would have received the highest score possible for this section of the test.

Immigration has been part of American life since colonial times. The immigrant left his or her homeland for many reasons, political, economic, religious and social. Once the immigrant arrived in the United States there were both positive and negative effects on the immigrant and on the country.

One of the positive effects immigration had on the immigrant was that through education the immigrant would be able to assimilate into the society. Document I reflects this as Chinese immigrants are being taught English in school. Another positive effect immigration had on the immigrant was that once the immigrant settled into the country there would be job opportunities. Document 3 points this out as the Americans in the cartoon believe that there would be jobs for the immigrants who came into this country.

One negative effect immigration had on the immigrant was that there was a language barrier the immigrant faced after entering the country. Another negative effect was that there was also prejudice shown by the nativists towards many immigrants. Document 5 points out that the Polish and Vietnamese-Cambodian immigrants faced similar problems. Both groups were at a disadvantage because they did not speak English. The document also pointed out that there were anti-immigrant statements made by Americans who did not like immigration. In fact throughout history the United States government passed many unfair immigration laws including the Chinese Exclusion Act in 1882 and immigration quotas in the 1920s.

One positive impact immigration had on life in the United States was that they offered the United States a cheap source of labor. Looking at Document 4, the Representative indicates the positive contribution the immigrant made in the coal mining and steel industries. Chinese laborers made a positive contribution helping to build the transcontinental railroad. Another positive effect immigrants had on life in the United States was that they offered the country many aspects of their own culture. The United States became a "melting pot" as a result of this. When you read Emma Lazarus' poem found in Document 7, it is clear that the Statue of Liberty is welcoming the immigrants to this country.

One negative effect immigration had on life in the United States was that many nativist groups reacted negatively towards immigrants and demanded that the government only allow those immigrants who had something to contribute to enter the country. Cartoon 2 in document 7 shows this as the cartoonist indicates that the United States should only allow immigrants who were educated and who had professions into the country. Another negative effect immigration had on life in the United States was that as a result of the cheap labor that immigrants provided some Americans lost their jobs to this new labor pool. This caused prejudice against the immigrants. Document 6 points this out as an angry mob is ready to attack the Chinese immigrant protected by Columbia.

Throughout the history of the United States immigrant groups arrived in this country. These groups included Chinese, European, Asian and people from Latin and South America. When many of the immigrants arrived they were greeted by the Statue of Liberty. After finding homes, immigrants faced a language barrier. The children entered school and education became a ticket to a better life. Immigrants also contributed to American life through their accomplishments. But there were also negatives. Nativists reacted to the immigrant and laws were passed restricting immigration. Many immigrants felt a prejudice. But in the end the United States became a large "melting pot."

Part III: Document-Based Question

Part B—Essay
Specific Scoring Rubric

5

- Thoroughly addresses all aspects of the Task (identifying and discussing the positive and negative effects of immigration and evaluating these effects by showing how immigration impacted the history of the United States) by accurately analyzing and interpreting at least four documents
- Places documents into a historical context by organizing documents into groupings such as reasons for immigration and the positive impact of immigration, and the reasons why people were against immigration, showing the negative effects of immigration
- Weaves information and ideas from the documents smoothly into the fabric of the essay by explaining how immigrants had both a positive and negative impact on life in the United States
- Incorporates relevant and useful outside information such as acts passed by Congress that restricted immigration (the Chinese-Exclusion Act and Immigration Quota Acts)
- Understands and effectively uses such key terms as immigration, melting pot, nativism, quotas
- Richly supports essay with relevant facts and examples such as details of the life of an immigrant and the obstacles an immigrant faced
- Shows an ability to discuss, describe, and explain the nature of immigration and its effects on life in the United States

- Writes a well-organized essay demonstrating a clear and logical plan of organization, with a balance of facts and analysis of the documents worked smoothly into the essay
- Introduces the Task with a framework that is beyond a simple restatement of the Task and concludes with a solid summary

4

- Addresses all aspects of the Task (identifying and discussing the positive and negative effects of immigration and evaluating these effects by showing how immigration impacted the history of the United States) by accurately analyzing and interpreting at least four documents
- Places documents into historical context by grouping the documents
- Incorporates relevant and useful outside information such as acts passed by Congress that restricted immigration (the Chinese-Exclusion Act and Immigration Quota Acts)
- Understands and effectively uses such key terms as immigration, melting pot, nativism, quotas
- Supports essay with relevant facts and examples in their proper historical context or setting, but the discussion may be more descriptive than analytical; for example, does not fully discuss the positive and negative aspects of immigration
- Shows an ability to discuss, describe, and explain the positive and negative aspects of immigration without the rich and full detail of a "5" answer
- Writes a well-organized essay demonstrating a clear and logical plan of organization; facts and analysis of the documents may be worked unevenly into the body of the essay
- Introduces the Task with a framework that is beyond a simple restatement of the Task and concludes with a solid summary

3

- Understands and addresses some aspects of the Task, or all aspects in a limited way by identifying and discussing some reasons why there were both positive and negative effects of immigration, and interpreting and using three of the documents
- Identifies and uses some relevant documents, incorporating them into the body of the essay

- Places some (but not all) documents into a historical context
- Incorporates little relevant and useful outside information, such as the context of how laws affected the flow of immigration
- Understands and uses some key terms, such as immigration and melting pot
- Supports essay with some relevant facts and examples in their proper historical context or setting, but the discussion is superficial
- Shows an ability to discuss, describe, and explain the immigration movement, but in a limited way and not in depth
- Writes a satisfactory essay demonstrating a general plan of organization with facts and description of the documents worked somewhat unevenly into the body of the essay
- Introduces the Task by repeating the Task or Historical Context (a simple restatement of the Task) and concludes by simply repeating the Task or Historical Context

2

- Attempts to address some aspects of the Task (identifying and discussing vague reasons why there were positive and negative effects of immigration) but with little use of the documents
- Includes few facts, examples, and details of the immigration movement; discussion only paraphrases the contents of documents
- Incorporates no relevant and useful outside information
- Uses key terms such as immigration and melting pot, but in a vague or incorrect manner
- Writes a poor essay, demonstrating a poor plan of organization, responding to only some parts of the Task; lacks focus
- Fails to introduce or summarize westward movement

1

- Shows very limited understanding of the Task, with unclear or no references to the documents
- Presents no relevant outside information about immigration
- Includes little or no accurate or relevant facts, details, or examples
- Understanding and use of key terms such as immigration or melting pot is vague or incorrect

- Writes a poor essay, demonstrating a major weakness in organization; lacks focus
- Has vague or inadequate introduction and conclusion

0
- Fails to address the Task, is illegible, or is a blank paper

MODEL EXAMINATION 2

PART I: MULTIPLE-CHOICE

Directions (1-45)

Each question is followed by four choices. Read each question carefully. Decide which choice is the correct answer. Mark your answer in the space provided.

1. Which item would provide an archaeologist with a primary source of information about pre-Columbian Indians who settled in New York?

   1. an article about the Iroquois in an encyclopedia
   2. an interview with a historian who specializes in early American cultures
   3. artifacts left by the Iroquois
   4. a social studies textbook

   1. _____

2. An important accomplishment of the Iroquois Confederacy was the

   1. establishment of a political union of member nations.
   2. adoption of a two-house legislature.
   3. selection of a woman as chief.
   4. development of a trading partnership with the Algonquin tribe.

   2. _____

3. One reason why groups of Native American Indians often developed different cultures was that each group

   1. came to America from other parts of the world.
   2. adapted to its environment in a different way.
   3. had to follow written traditions.
   4. wanted to be distinct from other groups.

   3. _____

4. Which is a primary source of evidence that Columbus sailed to find a new route to the Indies in 1492?

   1. a television show about the explorations of Columbus
   2. a letter from the current ambassador from Spain describing the voyage
   3. a painting showing Columbus landing in the New World
   4. a diary entry written by a crew member aboard Columbus' ship

   4. _____

5. During the period 1700 to 1770, the American colonial population increased from about 250,000 people to over 2,000,000. This growth of colonial society was mainly due to

   1. changes in the birthrate among the colonists.
   2. a sharp reduction of the colonial death rate.
   3. increased immigration from Europe.
   4. a rapid increase in the slave trade in the northern colonies.

   5. _____

6. Early colonists in North America tended to settle near rivers mainly because these areas provided

   1. resources suitable for agriculture.
   2. water power for factories.
   3. protection from enemies.
   4. popular camping sites.

   6. _____

7. Which statement identifies an outcome of the Treaty of Paris (1763) that ended the French and Indian War?

   1. Canada became a colony of Spain.
   2. The Dutch gave up New Netherlands to England.
   3. France lost most of its colonies in North America.
   4. Americans won their independence from the British.

   7. _____

8. In colonial America, an aim of British mercantile policy was to force American merchants to

   1. sell more raw materials to countries other than England.
   2. provide raw materials to England only.
   3. compete with England for overseas markets.
   4. produce all their own manufactured goods.

   8. _____

9. "Many of the [colonial] storekeepers couldn't give away any of the British goods on the stores' shelves. It was as if the colonists had agreed to not buy any English products."

   Which economic idea is described in this passage?

   1. a boycott
   2. a tariff
   3. a duty
   4. a strike

   9. _____

Base your answer to question 10 on the speakers' statements below and on your knowledge of social studies.

Speaker A:
"I would have hanged my brother if he took part with our enemy in this country," said patriot Sam Adams.

Speaker B:
"Bodies were then piled in the carts and hauled through the streets. The Loyalists laughed and hooted as they saw these carts go by. 'There goes another load of rebels,' they would say."

10. Based on these statements, which conclusion can best be drawn about the colonists' support for independence from England?

   1. Patriots received better treatment than Loyalists received.
   2. Patriots and Loyalists both wanted to end British rule of the colonies.
   3. All American colonists favored independence from England.
   4. The issue of independence from England caused sharp differences among the American colonists.

   10. _____

11. A basic idea stated by Thomas Jefferson in the Declaration of Independence is that

   1. the power to govern a nation comes from the people.
   2. people should always follow their government.
   3. America must have a constitutional convention.
   4. slavery must end in America.

   11. _____

12. A major argument against ratification of the United States Constitution in 1787 was that it

   1. gave too much power to state governments.
   2. was not based on compromises.
   3. did not contain a bill of rights.
   4. established a legislative branch of government.

   12. _____

13. The dispute over representation in Congress between large and small states was settled in the United States Constitution by

   1. adopting the Three-Fifths Compromise.
   2. establishing the reserved powers.
   3. creating a two-house legislature.
   4. forming the electoral college.

   13. _____

14. The United States Constitution established a government based on the basic concepts of separation of powers and checks and balances. The authors of the Constitution included these two concepts because they

   1. give most of the power to the executive branch.
   2. were contained in the Articles of Confederation.
   3. ensure that government branches would operate without disagreement.
   4. prevent any one branch of government from becoming too powerful.

   14. _____

15. The elastic clause and the amending procedure in the United States Constitution have often been used to

   1. allow the government to adjust to changing times.
   2. give more power to the president.
   3. limit the role of minorities in government.
   4. limit democracy in the United States.

   15. _____

16. The New York State Assembly is most similar to the

    1. British Parliament.
    2. United States Senate.
    3. United States House of Representatives.
    4. Canadian House of Lords.

16. _____

17. In pre-industrial New York State, yearly agricultural activities were organized mainly around

    1. major patriotic holidays.
    2. celebrations of peace and war.
    3. cycles of work and rest.
    4. periods determined by nature.

17. _____

18. The Seneca Falls Convention of 1848 was called to focus attention on

    1. women's rights.
    2. slavery.
    3. public education.
    4. the abuse of alcohol.

18. _____

19. Which author's work gave support to the Abolitionist movement before the Civil War?

    1. Upton Sinclair's *The Jungle*
    2. Margaret Mitchell's *Gone With the Wind*
    3. Booker T. Washington's *Up From Slavery*
    4. Harriet Beecher Stowe's *Uncle Tom's Cabin*

19. _____

Base your answer to question 20 on the graphs below and on your knowledge of social studies.

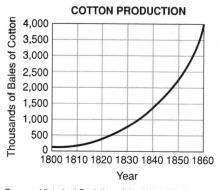

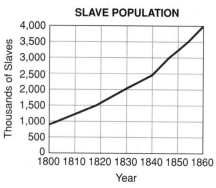

20. What was the relationship between cotton production and the slave population?

   1. To produce more cotton, more slaves were needed.
   2. An increase in the slave population resulted in a decrease in cotton production.
   3. To produce more cotton, fewer slaves were needed.
   4. Cotton production had little effect on the slave population.

   20. _____

21. As a result of Abraham Lincoln's election as president in 1860, several Southern states called for

   1. another vote by the electoral college.
   2. the House of Representatives to choose a president.
   3. secession from the Union.
   4. a constitutional amendment ending slavery.

   21. _____

22. President Abraham Lincoln's main goal throughout the Civil War was to

    1. abolish slavery throughout the nation.
    2. preserve the Union.
    3. break the South's dependence on cotton.
    4. end British control of the western territories.

    22. _____

23. Which statement best describes the political situation of African-Americans in the South after Reconstruction ended in 1877?

    1. They gained more seats in state legislatures.
    2. They lost interest in politics and government.
    3. They formed political parties, which became strong and influential.
    4. They had little political power because of restrictions on voting rights.

    23. _____

24. The completion of the Transcontinental Railroad in 1869 contributed to the settlement of which United States region?

    1. Northeast
    2. West
    3. South
    4. Southeast

    24. _____

25. In the late 1800s, the increase in the number of tenement buildings resulted directly from the

    1. rapid growth of urban populations.
    2. need for health care facilities.
    3. increased federal aid for housing.
    4. changing role of women in the home.

    25. _____

26. Which development was a result of the other three?

    1. young children working in factories
    2. unsafe working conditions
    3. the growth of labor unions
    4. a twelve-hour workday

    26. _____

27. Which statement best describes United States economic history during the period 1865 to 1900?

    1. Industrialization increased at a rapid rate.
    2. Factories imported most of their raw materials.
    3. The lack of immigration tended to decrease industrial production.
    4. American industrial technology was hindered by the Civil War.

    27. _____

28. Corporations, stocks, and trusts are most closely connected with the

    1. rise of big business.
    2. development of the factory system.
    3. formation of labor unions.
    4. invention of the automobile.

    28. _____

29. The idea of Manifest Destiny meant that
    1. Native Americans had an equal claim to the lands of the West.
    2. slavery should be allowed in the West.
    3. no more European colonies would be allowed in the Americas.
    4. the United States had the right to expand to the Pacific Ocean.

    29. _____

30. Which development in Europe was a result of the other three?

    1. growth of intense nationalism
    2. outbreak of World War I
    3. power struggles between nations
    4. Formation of alliances

30. _____

Base your answer to question 31 on the poster below and on your knowledge of social studies.

31. What is the main idea of this poster?

    1. Prohibition was a major goal for the United States during World War I.
    2. Patriotic appeals were used to gain support for the Prohibition movement.
    3. Many soldiers in the United States military had a drinking problem.
    4. Trench warfare on the western front led to large casualty and death rates.

31. _____

32. Many Americans were opposed to the United States joining the League of Nations because they believed that the

    1. dues the United States would pay would be too costly.
    2. League of Nations would not be based on democratic principles.
    3. League of Nations would allow Germany to join.
    4. United States might become involved in another European war.

    32. _____

33. Which event is credited with starting the Great Depression?

    1. the election of Franklin D. Roosevelt as president
    2. the stock market crash
    3. the Senate's failure to ratify the Treaty of Versailles
    4. the adoption of the New Deal

    33. _____

34. According to the law of supply and demand, farmers will obtain the highest price for their products when

    1. both supply and demand are high.
    2. both supply and demand are low.
    3. supply is high and demand is low.
    4. supply is low and demand is high.

    34. _____

35. The New Deal period in American history is associated with the idea that

    1. people are responsible for their own success or failure.
    2. churches and charities do the best job of helping the poor.
    3. government must take responsibility for helping those in need.
    4. local governments are best equipped to take care of their own citizens.

    35. _____

36. Which event caused Britain and France to declare war on Germany in 1939?

    1. the signing of the Munich Settlement
    2. the invasion of Poland
    3. an alliance with the Soviet Union
    4. the bombing of London

    36. _____

37. European Jews and other groups were killed in large numbers by Nazi Germany during World War II. Which term refers to this situation?

    1. appeasement
    2. *Blitzkrieg*
    3. containment
    4. Holocaust

    37. _____

38. During the Cold War, the United States used the policy of containment to limit the spread of

    1. parliamentary democracy.
    2. absolute monarchy.
    3. communism.
    4. fascism.

    38. _____

39. One reason many Americans opposed United States involvement in the war in Vietnam was that

    1. communism should be allowed to spread in Asia.
    2. the conflict was considered a civil war and did not concern the United States.
    3. the conflict should be resolved by the Soviet Union.
    4. the war was causing problems for Europe.

    39. _____

40. The *Brown* v. *Board of Education* decision, the Montgomery bus boycott, and the 1963 March on Washington were all efforts to

   1. protect freedom of speech as guaranteed by the Bill of Rights.
   2. guarantee civil rights to all citizens of the United States.
   3. promote economic reform.
   4. end the persecution of the McCarthy era.

   40. _____

41. Which statement is supported by the information in the timeline?

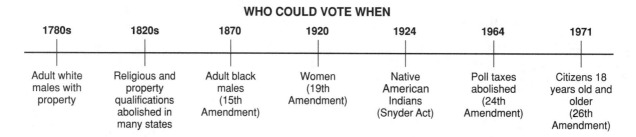

   1. All Americans have had the right to vote since the nation was established.
   2. Very few Americans who have the right to vote do so in national elections.
   3. The right to vote has been gradually extended.
   4. Voters today make wiser choices about political candidates.

   41. _____

42. "Although women gained the right to vote in 1920, it wasn't until 1984 that former Congresswoman Geraldine Ferraro became the first woman to run for Vice President of the United States."

   The author of this statement is probably trying to point out that

   1. women were not allowed to seek a high office before the 1980s.
   2. the attitudes of the American people are difficult to change.
   3. before 1984 women did not want to be vice president.
   4. before 1984 few women had experience in Congress.

   42. _____

43. This political cartoon best illustrates the concept of

1. secession.
2. Prohibition.
3. imperialism.
4. communism.

43. _____

44. Sectionalism in the United States contributed most to the start of the

1. labor union movement.
2. Great Depression.
3. Industrial Revolution.
4. Civil War.

44. _____

45. The terms deficit spending, debtor nation status, and trade imbalance refer to

1. social problems.
2. economic problems.
3. racial problems.
4. environmental problems.

45. _____

PART II: CONSTRUCTED RESPONSE QUESTIONS

Directions (1-15)

For each question, write your answer in the space provided. You may use either pen or pencil to write your answers. If you want to change an answer, cross out or erase your original response. You may not know the answers to some of the questions, but do the best you can on each one.

I. Base your answers to questions 1–3 on the map below and on your knowledge of social studies.

BUILDING OF THE ERIE CANAL

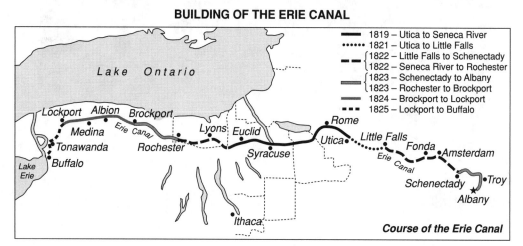

1. What is the subject of the map?

_____

_____ (1)

2. What was the first year that goods could be shipped between Albany and Buffalo on the Erie Canal?

_____

_____ (1)

3. What is one major impact of the Erie Canal on the growth of the United States?

_____

_____ (2)

II. Base your answers to questions 4–6 on the poster below, which was published shortly after the Fugitive Slave Act of 1850 was passed, and on your knowledge of social studies.

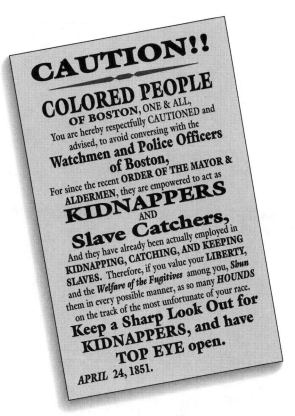

4. What group is being warned by this poster?

_____

_____ (1)

5. Why are these people being warned?

_____

_____ (2)

6. What group was most likely responsible for publishing this poster?

_____

_____ (1)

III. Base your answers to questions 7–11 on the telegram below and on your knowledge of social studies.

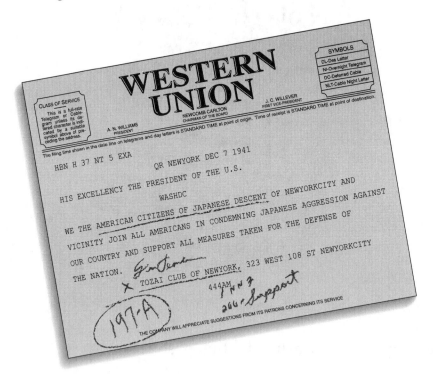

7. What group sent this telegram to the president?

_____

_____ (1)

8. To which United States president was this telegram sent?

_____

_____ (1)

9. What major event happened on the day the telegram was sent?

_____

_____ (1)

10. Why would those who sent the telegram be concerned about something Japan did to the United States?

_____

_____ (1)

11. Why did those who sent the telegram have reason to worry?

_____

_____ (1)

IV. Base your answers to questions 12–15 on the chart below and your knowledge of social studies.

ANNUAL EARNINGS, BY EDUCATION ATTAINMENT, SEX, RACE, AND HISPANIC ORIGIN, 1992
AVERAGES PER PERSON

Characteristic	Total	Not a high school graduate	High school graduate	Four-year college degree	Advanced degree
Total	$23,277	$12,809	$18,737	$32,629	$48,653
Male	28,448	14,934	22,978	40,039	58,324
Female	17,145	9,311	14,128	23,991	33,814
White	23,932	13,193	19,265	33,092	49,346
Black	17,416	11,077	15,260	27,457	39,088
Hispanic origin[1]	16,824	11,836	16,714	28,260	41,297

Source: *Bureau of the Census, U.S. Dept. of Commerce*   [1]May be of any race

12. What is the source of this chart?

_____

_____ (1)

13. According to the chart, which group at which level of education was paid the lowest average annual earning?

_____

_____ (2)

14. What does this chart show about the annual earnings of males and females in the United States population in 1992?

_____

_____ (1)

15. State one generalization about the relationship between level of education and level of income for the total number of Americans in 1992.

_____

_____ (2)

PART III: DOCUMENT-BASED QUESTION

Generic Scoring Rubric

5

- ■ Thoroughly addresses all aspects of the Task by accurately analyzing and interpreting at least four documents
- ■ Incorporates information from the documents in the body of the essay
- ■ Incorporates relevant outside information
- ■ Richly supports the theme or problem with relevant facts, examples, and details
- ■ Is a well-developed essay, consistently demonstrating a logical and clear plan of organization
- ■ Introduces the theme or problem by establishing a framework that is beyond a simple restatement of the Task or Historical Context and concludes with a summation of the theme or problem

4

- ■ Addresses all aspects of the Task by accurately analyzing and interpreting at least four documents
- ■ Incorporates information from the documents in the body of the essay
- ■ Incorporates relevant outside information
- ■ Includes relevant facts, examples, and details, but discussion may be more descriptive than analytical
- ■ Is a well-developed essay, demonstrating a logical and clear plan of organization
- ■ Introduces the theme or problem by establishing a framework that is beyond a simple restatement of the Task or Historical Context and concludes with a summation of the theme or problem

3

- Addresses most aspects of the Task or addresses all aspects of the Task in a limited way, using some of the documents
- Incorporates some information from the documents in the body of the essay
- Incorporates limited or no relevant outside information
- Includes some facts, examples, and details, but discussion is more descriptive than analytical
- Is a satisfactorily developed essay, demonstrating a general plan of organization
- Introduces the theme or problem by repeating the Task or Historical Context and concludes by simply repeating the theme or problem

2

- Attempts to address some aspects of the Task, making limited use of the documents
- Presents no relevant outside information
- Includes few facts, examples, and details; discussion restates contents of the documents
- Is a poorly organized essay, lacking focus
- Fails to introduce or summarize the theme or problem

1

- Shows limited understanding of the Task with vague, unclear references to the documents
- Presents no relevant outside information
- Includes little or no accurate or relevant facts, details, or examples
- Attempts to complete the Task, but demonstrates a major weakness in organization
- Fails to introduce or summarize the theme or problem

0

- Fails to address the Task, is illegible, or is a blank paper

Part III: Document-Based Question

This question is based on the accompanying documents (1–7). Some of the documents have been edited for the purpose of the question. The question is designed to test your ability to work with historical documents. As you analyze the documents, take into account both the context of each document and any point of view that may be presented in the document.

Directions: This document-based question consists of two parts. Be sure to put the booklet number at the top of each page. Use black or dark ink to answer the question.

Historical Context
In the second half of the nineteenth century, the United States became an increasingly mobile society. An example of this mobility is the settlement of the West by easterners. For many Americans, the movement westward brought new economic opportunities, but for others it meant conflict and the end of a way of life.

Task
Using information from the documents and your knowledge of social studies, answer the questions that follow each document in Part A. Your answers to the questions will help you write the Part B essay in which you will be asked to:

- Identify and discuss two reasons settlers moved westward.
- Describe the impact of railroads on the West.
- Explain the impact of this westward movement on the lives of Native American Indians.

Part A—Short Answer
Directions: Analyze the documents and answer the questions that follow each document in the space provided. Your answers to questions will help you write the essay.

Document 1: Illustration of a woman from the Dakota tribe preparing a buffalo hide.

© Bettmann/CORBIS

1. Based on this illustration and caption, what evidence is there that buffaloes were important to Native American Indians?

_____

_____ (2)

Document 2: "Crossing Over the Great Plains by Ox-Wagon."

Although I was but a girl of 11 years I distinctly remember many things connected with that far-off time when all of our western country was a wilderness ... We were six months in crossing the plains in ox-wagons. In our home, in Illinois, in the early fifties, there was much talk and excitement over the news of the great gold discoveries in California—and equally there was much talk concerning the wonderful fertile valleys of Oregon Territory—an act of Congress giving to actual settlers 640 acres of land. My father, John Tucker Scott, with much of the pioneer spirit in his blood, became so interested that he decided to "go West" . . . The spring of 1852 ushered in so many preparations, great work of all kinds. I remember relations coming to sew, of tearful partings, little gifts of remembrances exchanged, the sale of the farm, the buying and breaking in of unruly oxen, the loud voices of the men, and the general confusion.

Harriet Scott Palmer, 1852

2. According to the document, what were two reasons people wanted to "Go West"?

_____

_____ (2)

Document 3: A Homestead Deed.

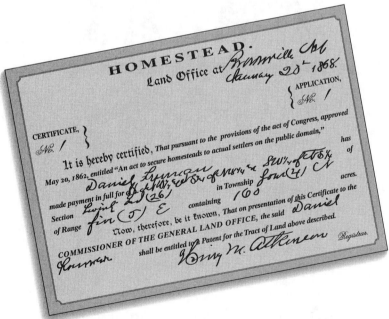

3. According to this deed, how many acres of land did each homesteader obtain from the government under the Homestead Act?

_____

_____ (1)

Document 4: Union Pacific Railway poster.

© CORBIS

4. Based on this poster, state two reasons people took passage on the railroad from Omaha to San Francisco.

_____

_____ (2)

Document 5: Illustration of a buffalo hunt.

© CORBIS

5a. According to this illustration, why were men killing buffalo?

_____

_____ (1)

5b. How did this purpose for hunting differ from those of Native American Indians? (See also Document 1.)

_____

_____ (2)

Document 6: Grand Rush poster.

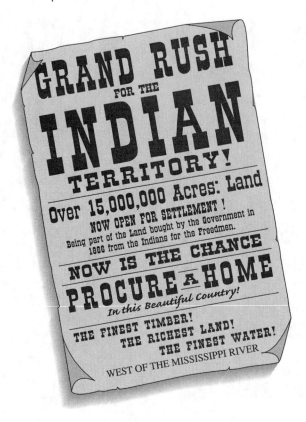

6a. According to this poster, how many acres of former Indian territory were going to be opened for settlement?

_____

_____ (1)

6b. Based on the poster, state two reasons settlers would want to move west of the Mississippi.

_____

_____ (1)

Document 7: Surrender of Chief Joseph.

I am tired of fighting. Our chiefs are killed ... He who led the young men is dead. It is cold and we have no blankets. The little children are freezing to death. My people, some of them have run away to the hills and have no blankets, no food; no one knows where they are—perhaps freezing to death. I want to have time to look for my children and see how many I can find. Maybe I shall find them among the dead. Hear me my chiefs. I am tired; my heart is sick and sad. From where the sun now stands, I will fight no more forever.

> Chief Joseph of the Nez Perce, upon his surrender to
> U.S. government troops,
> September 1877

7. Based on this statement, state two reasons Chief Joseph finally decided to surrender to the United States government troops.

_____

_____ (2)

Part B—Essay

Directions:

- Write a well-organized essay that includes an introduction, several paragraphs, and a conclusion.
- Use evidence from the documents to support your response.
- Include specific related outside information.
- Use black or dark ink to write your essay.

Historical Context

In the second half of the nineteenth century, the United States became an increasingly mobile society. An example of this mobility is the settlement of the West by easterners. For many Americans, the movement westward brought new economic opportunities, but for others it meant conflict and the end of a way of life.

Task

Using information from the documents and your knowledge of social studies, answer the questions that follow each document in Part A. Your answers to the questions will help you write the Part B essay in which you will be asked to:

- Identify and discuss two reasons settlers moved westward.
- Describe the impact of railroads on the West.
- Explain the impact of this westward movement on the lives of Native American Indians.

Be sure to include specific historical details. You must also include additional information from your knowledge of social studies.

MODEL EXAMINATION 2 ANSWERS

Part I: Multiple-Choice Answer Key

Please note that the Roman numeral next to the answer represents the scope and sequence Unit and the Arabic number represents the Standard. (See chart below).

1.	3	I-1	16.	3	IV-5	31.	2	VIII-1
2.	1	I-5	17.	4	V-3	32.	4	VIII-1
3.	2	I-3	18.	1	V-5	33.	2	IX-4
4.	4	II-1	19.	4	V-1	34.	4	IX-4
5.	3	II-3	20.	1	V-4	35.	3	IX-1
6.	1	II-3	21.	3	VI-1	36.	2	X-2
7.	3	III-2	22.	2	VI-5	37.	4	X-2
8.	2	III-4	23.	4	VI-5	38.	3	X-1
9.	1	III-4	24.	2	VII-3	39.	2	X-1
10.	4	III-1	25.	1	VII-1	40.	2	XI-1
11.	1	III-5	26.	3	VII-1	41.	3	XI-5
12.	3	IV-1	27.	1	VII-4	42.	1	XI-5
13.	3	IV-5	28.	1	VII-4	43.	3	CT-1
14.	4	IV-5	29.	4	VIII-3	44.	4	CT-1
15.	1	IV-5	30.	2	VIII-1	45.	2	CT-4

GRADE EIGHT INTERMEDIATE SOCIAL STUDIES TEST SPECIFICATIONS GRID
MULTIPLE-CHOICE ITEMS BY STANDARD AND UNIT

Standard → ↓ Unit	1 US and NY History	2 World History	3 Geography	4 Economics	5 Civics, Citizen- ship, and Government	Number
1–Prior to 1500	1	0	3	0	2	3
2–Exploration/Colonization	4	0	5, 6	0	0	3
3–A Nation Created	10	7	0	8, 9	11	5
4–Experiment in Government	12	0	0	0	13, 14, 15, 16	5
5–Life in a New Nation	19	0	17	20	18	4
6–Division and Reunion	21	0	0	0	22, 23	3
7–An Industrial Society	25, 26	0	24	27, 28	0	5
8–An Interdependent World	30, 31, 32	0	29	0	0	4
9–Between the Wars	35	0	0	33, 34	0	3
10–Worldwide Responsibilities	36, 39	36, 37	0	0	0	4
11–WW II to the Present	40	0	0	0	41, 42	3
11*–Cross-Topical	33, 43	0	0	45	0	3
Total						45

*Items placed in row 11 are cross-topical. Cross-topical items address content from two or more units.

Part I: Multiple-Choice Answers Explained

1. **3** Artifacts left by the Iroquois would provide an archeologist with a primary source of information about pre-Columbian Indians who settled in New York. Primary sources of information provide evidence of a particular event and are created at the time of the event in question. Relics left by the Iroquois, such as the tools they used, would be a primary source of information for an archeologist studying pre-Columbian Indians.

Wrong Choices Explained:
(1) An article about the Iroquois in an encyclopedia may be accurate, but it is not a primary source. An encyclopedia article is based on other, second-hand, sources.
(2) An interview with a historian who specializes in early American cultures is a good second-hand source but is not a primary source of information.
(4) A social studies textbook is a compilation of facts about different eras of history. It may include replicas of primary documents or pictures of artifacts, but it is not a primary source.

2. **1** An important accomplishment of the Iroquois Confederacy, formed in 1570, was the establishment of a political union between the Cayuga, Mohawk, Oneida, Onondaga, and Seneca tribes and, later, the Tuscarora Indian nation.

Wrong Choices Explained:
(2) The Iroquois Confederacy did not adopt any form of legislative body.
(3) Even though women held positions of authority, the Iroquois Confederacy never selected a woman as chief.
(4) The Iroquois Confederacy never entered into a trade partnership with the Algonquin tribe.

3. **2** A major reason why different cultures developed among the various tribes of Native Americans was that each tribe adapted to their environment in different ways. Native American tribes lived in geographically diverse areas, which affected the way each tribe lived, hunted, and so on. For instance the Nootka, Kwakiutl, and Haida lived on the Northwest coast, located along the Pacific Ocean from Alaska to northern California. The

Yakima, Paleuse, and Walla Walla lived in the plateau area covering eastern Washington, Oregon, and the Northwest. The Anasazi, Pueblo, Hopi, and eventually, the Apache and Navajo tribes lived in the Southwest.

Wrong Choices Explained:

(1) It is commonly believed that Native Americans originally came from Asia via a land bridge. Therefore, the statement that different cultures developed as a result of tribes coming from different areas of the world is incorrect.

(3) While different tribes had their own written traditions, the major reason why tribes developed different cultures was that they settled in different geographical areas that affected life in each tribe in different ways.

(4) The major reason why different cultures developed among the tribes of Native Americans was that each tribe had to adapt to their geographic locations, not because the tribes wanted to be distinct.

4. **4** A diary entry written by a crew member aboard Columbus' ship would be a primary source of evidence that Columbus sailed to find a new route to the Indies. A primary source is material that comes directly from the historical time period at issue. In this case, the only direct evidence from the time of Columbus' voyage is the diary entry of someone aboard his ship.

Wrong Choices Explained:

(1) A television show about the explorations of Columbus might be based on primary sources of information, but the actual television show, made centuries later, is not first-hand evidence.

(2) A letter from the current ambassador from Spain describing the voyage is a current interpretation of the actual event and is, therefore, not a primary document.

(3) A painting of Columbus landing in the New World is not primary evidence that Columbus sailed to the New World in order to find a new route to the Indies.

5. **3** The significant increase in the colonial population between 1700 to 1770 was the direct result of the increased number of people who came to the New World from Europe.

Wrong Choices Explained:

(1) While changes in the birthrate among colonists might explain some of the population increase, it alone could not explain the enormous increase in the colonial population.

(2) While a sharp reduction in the colonial death rate might explain some of the population increase, it alone could not explain the enormous increase in the colonial population.

(4) Although there was a rapid increase in the slave trade, it did not take place in the northern colonies.

6. **1** Early American colonists tended to settle near rivers mainly because these areas provided resources suitable for agriculture such as fertile soil, means of irrigation, and a method of transportation.

Wrong Choices Explained:

(2) Early colonists did not tend to settle near rivers because they provided water power for factories because the factory system did not develop until the 1800s.

(3) Rivers did not provide protection because they were a means for a hostile nation to attack settlements.

(4) Early colonists did not settle near rivers because they provided popular camping sites.

7. **3** The Treaty of Paris, in 1763, ending the French and Indian War, resulted in Great Britain acquiring Canada and the rest of the lands east of the Mississippi River from France. Since Spain helped France during the war, Great Britain also received Florida from Spain.

Wrong Choices Explained:

(1) Canada became a colony of Great Britain, not Spain.

(2) The Dutch did not give up New Netherlands to England as a result of the war.

(4) Americans won their independence from Great Britain as a result of the American Revolution, not the French and Indian War.

8. **2** The aim of the British mercantile policy was to benefit Great Britain by forcing colonial merchants to provide raw materials to England exclusively.

Wrong Choices Explained:

(1) Under the British mercantile policy, the colonies were not allowed to sell raw materials to other countries except England.

(3) The colonies were not allowed to compete with England for overseas markets under the British mercantile policy.

(4) Under the British mercantile policy, very little manufactured goods were produced by the colonists.

9. **1** The economic idea described in the passage is a boycott of British goods. The passage refers to the decision made by colonists to refuse to purchase British goods.

Wrong Choices Explained:

(2) A tariff is a tax imposed on imported goods.

(3) A duty is a tax on imported goods, usually raw materials.

(4) A strike is a tool used by labor unions designed to pressure employers into negotiations by calling for a work stoppage by its members.

10. **4** Based on these statements, the best conclusion that can be drawn about the colonists' support for independence from England was that the issue caused sharp differences among the colonists. Each statement reflects a strong feeling for and against American independence. Those in favor of independence were known as patriots, while those in favor of British rule were known as Loyalists.

Wrong Choices Explained:

(1) Loyalists supported British rule, and, therefore, received much better treatment at the hands of British officials.

(2) Loyalists did not want an end to British rule of the colonies.

(3) Loyalists were American colonists who did not want independence from England. Use of the absolute word *all* is a hint that this is a wrong choice.

11. **1** A basic idea stated by Jefferson in the Declaration of Independence was that the power to govern comes from the people. The purpose of the Declaration of Independence was to inform Great Britain and the rest of the world why the colonists wanted their freedom. In the introduction, Jefferson outlined the belief that a government needed the consent of the people to rule.

Wrong Choices Explained:

(2) The belief that people should always follow their government is not a basic idea contained in the Declaration of Independence. The use of the absolute word *always* is a hint that this is a wrong choice.

(3) The need for a constitutional convention is not a basic idea contained in the Declaration of Independence. A constitutional convention was not held until 1789, after the Articles of Confederation failed.

(4) The notion that slavery should be abolished is not a basic idea contained in the Declaration of Independence.

12. **3** A major argument against ratification of the U.S. Constitution in 1787 was that it did not contain a bill of rights. The new Constitution created a balance of power between the federal and state governments, known as federalism. Many people feared that the new federal government would be too powerful and, that without a bill of rights guaranteeing the rights of citizens, the federal government would be able to deny people their basic liberties.

Wrong Choices Explained:

(1) The Articles of Confederation, not the U.S. Constitution, was criticized for giving too much power to the state governments.

(2) The U.S. Constitution was based on a series of compromises including the Great Compromise and the Three-Fifths Compromise.

(4) Establishment of a legislative branch, consisting of the Senate and House of Representatives, was not a major argument against ratification of the Constitution.

13. **3** The dispute over representation in Congress was settled by the adoption of the Great Compromise. Various plans for establishing representation caused debate among the states. The New Jersey plan called for a one-house legislature based on equal representation among the states. The Virginia plan favored larger states by calling for a legislature with representation based on state population. Representatives from Connecticut came up with a compromise, which became known as the Great Compromise, that created two houses, a Senate, with equal representation, and a House of Representatives, with representation based on the population.

Wrong Choices Explained:

(1) The Three-Fifths Compromise settled the dispute over how to count slaves for purposes of representation. Under the compromise, every five slaves counted as three people for representation purposes.

(2) The dispute over representation was not settled by the establishment of the reserved powers. The reserved powers are part of the Tenth Amendment to the Constitution and guarantee that the states have all powers not given to the federal government.

(4) The dispute over representation was not settled by the formation of the electoral college. The electoral college was established as a mechanism for electing the president, not for apportioning representation in the Congress.

14. **4** The authors of the Constitution included the concepts of separation of powers and checks and balances because they wanted to prevent any one branch of government from becoming too powerful. The separation of powers, which divides the federal government into three branches, each with specific powers, and the system of checks and balances, whereby each branch of the federal government has the ability to review the actions of the other branches, acts as a limitation on power and prevents any one branch from becoming too powerful.

Wrong Choices Explained:

(1) Separation of powers and checks and balances distributes federal power among the three branches. They do not concentrate powers in the executive branch of government.

(2) The concepts of separation of powers and checks and balances were not contained in the Articles of Confederation. The authors of the Constitution wanted to avoid the problems associated with the Articles of Confederation, one of which was that the Articles of Confederation gave most of the power to state governments.

(3) The concepts of separation of powers and checks and balances were not included in the Constitution to ensure that the branches of government would operate without disagreement. They were included to prevent any one branch from becoming too powerful.

15. **1** The elastic clause, also called the "necessary and proper" clause, and the amending procedure in the Constitution have often been used to

allow the government to adjust to changing times. The elastic clause enables Congress to "stretch" its powers in order to adapt to changing times. For instance, when originally written the Constitution gave Congress the power to support an army and a navy. Congress created the air force, by using the elastic clause to "stretch" its power to support an army and a navy and to also support an air force. The amending procedure of the Constitution serves a similar purpose. When the need arises, the Constitution may be changed through the adoption of an amendment.

Wrong Choices Explained:
    (2) The elastic clause and amending procedure do not give more power to the president.
    (3) The elastic clause and amending procedure do not limit the role of minorities in government. In fact, they have been used to expand civil rights. For instance, Congress passed the Civil Rights Act of 1964 using the elastic clause and the Thirteenth, Fourteenth, and Fifteenth Amendments were enacted to extend the rights of citizenship to freed slaves.
    (4) The elastic clause and amending procedure do not limit democracy.

16. **3** The New York State Assembly is most similar to the U.S. House of Representatives. Both the State Assembly and the U.S. House of Representatives base representation on population.

Wrong Choices Explained:
    (1) The British House of Parliament is a legislative body wherein representation is based on the number of votes a political party receives in an election.
    (2) Representation in the U.S. Senate is based on equal representation, with every state receiving two senators.
    (4) The Canadian House of Lords is an appointed body.

17. **4** In pre-industrial New York, yearly agricultural activities were organized mainly around periods determined by nature. Before the Industrial Revolution, New York State's economy was heavily dependent on agriculture. Agricultural activities, like planting and harvesting, therefore, had to be organized based upon the environment and weather patterns.

Wrong Choices Explained:

(1) Major patriotic holidays did not have an affect on agricultural activities.

(2) Celebrations of peace and war did not have an affect on agricultural activities.

(3) While cycles of work and rest would be factors in the organization of agricultural activities, these cycles are based on the environment and weather patterns. Farmers would work in the warmer weather, planting and harvesting, and rest in the colder weather.

18. **1** The Seneca Falls Convention of 1848 was called to focus attention on women's rights. The convention was organized by women right's activists Elizabeth Cady Stanton and Lucretia Mott. The convention adopted a "Declaration of Sentiments" that sought greater women's rights including better employment opportunities, increased wages, better educational opportunities, and a resolution calling for the right of women to vote.

Wrong Choices Explained:

(2) The Seneca Falls Convention was not called to focus attention on slavery.

(3) The Seneca Falls Convention was not called to focus attention on public education.

(4) The Seneca Falls Convention was not called to focus attention on the abuse of alcohol.

19. **4** Harriet Beecher Stowe's *Uncle Tom's Cabin,* published in 1852, was a fictional work dealing with the way slaves were treated and gave support to the Abolitionist movement before the Civil War.

Wrong Choices Explained:

(1) Upton Sinclair's *The Jungle,* published in 1906, was about abuses in the meatpacking industry.

(2) Margaret Mitchell's *Gone With the Wind* was a novel dealing with the Civil War but was published after the Civil War.

(3) Booker T. Washington's *Up From Slavery* was a biographical novel depicting Washington's life as a slave. However, it was published after the Civil War.

20. **1** Based on the two graphs, in order to produce more cotton, more slaves were needed. In 1820 one million slaves were producing five hundred thousand bales of cotton. By 1860, four million slaves were needed to produce four million bales of cotton. As the number of bales of cotton increased, the number of slaves also increased in order to keep up with the production.

Wrong Choices Explained:
   (2) The graphs do not support this choice because they show that as more cotton was produced more slaves were needed, and, therefore, the slave population grew.
   (3) The graphs do not support this choice because they show that cotton production and the slave population both grew.
   (4) The graphs clearly indicate that cotton production did have an effect on the slave population. As cotton production increased, an increase in the slave population was needed in order to account for the increased production.

21. **3** As a result of Lincoln's election in 1860, several Southern states called for secession from the Union because they feared he would abolish slavery. A number of Southern states, including South Carolina, did secede and the Civil War began in 1861.

Wrong Choices Explained:
   (1) Southern states did not call for another vote by the electoral college.
   (2) Southern states did not call for the House of Representatives to choose a president. The U.S. House of Representatives only does so when a candidate does not get a majority of electoral votes.
   (4) Southern states did not call for a constitutional amendment ending slavery. Southern states feared Lincoln would abolish slavery and, therefore, seceded from the Union.

22. **2** Although slavery was an underlying cause of the Civil War, Lincoln's main goal throughout the conflict was to preserve the Union. In fact, his Emancipation Proclamation, issued during the Civil War, only abolished slavery in the Southern states that left the Union. It did not free slaves in border states that remained loyal to the Union. Slavery was abolished after the Civil War, when the Thirteenth Amendment was ratified.

Wrong Choices Explained:

(1) Lincoln's main goal throughout the Civil War was to preserve the Union.

(3) Lincoln's main goal was not to break the South's dependency on cotton.

(4) British control of the Western territories had already ended by the time the Civil War began, and, therefore, was not Lincoln's main goal throughout the conflict.

23. **4** The statement that best describes the political situation of African-Americans in the South after Reconstruction is that they had little political power because of restrictions on their voting rights. During Reconstruction, Congress established a method for allowing Southern states back into the Union. As part of that method, the Southern states had to recognize that former slaves were guaranteed their freedom by the Thirteenth Amendment, that they were given citizenship rights including equal protection under the law by the Fourteenth Amendment, and that they were given the right to vote by the Fifteenth Amendment. However, many Southern states passed laws such as literacy acts, which required a person to be able to read in order to vote, and poll taxes, which required a person to pay in order to vote. The impact of these laws resulted in little political power for African-Americans.

Wrong Choices Explained:

(1) Because freed slaves could not exercise the voting rights given to them, they were not able to gain seats in state legislatures.

(2) African-Americans, although unable to exercise the rights given to them, did not lose interest in politics and government.

(3) African-Americans did not form their own political parties. Traditionally, African-Americans have been strong supporters of the Democratic Party.

24. **2** The completion of the Transcontinental Railroad in 1869 contributed to the settlement of the West. The joining of the Central Pacific Railroad and the Union Pacific Railroad at Promontory Point, Utah opened the western frontier and encouraged the settlement of the West. The Homestead Act, passed in 1862, opened up western lands to settlers, and the railroad played a key role in providing a means for the pioneers to move out west.

Wrong Choices Explained:

(1) The Transcontinental Railroad did not contribute to the settlement of the Northeast.

(3) The Transcontinental Railroad did not contribute to the settlement of the South.

(4) The Transcontinental Railroad did not contribute to the settlement of the Southeast.

25. **1** In the late 1800s, the increase in the number of tenement buildings resulted directly from the rapid growth of urban populations. As immigration and birthrates increased, cities began to grow. As the size of cities grew the need for housing also grew. Tenement housing, low-cost and often substandard apartment houses, were built to meet this housing need. Although tenement houses provided shelter, they were often overcrowded, unsanitary, and dangerous places to live. Jacob Riis wrote about the poor living conditions of tenement housing in his famous book, *How the Other Half Lives*.

Wrong Choices Explained:

(2) The increase in the number of tenement buildings did not result from the need for health care facilities. Like the tenements, the need for health care facilities resulted from the rapid growth of urban populations.

(3) During the late 1800s, federal aid for housing was not available.

(4) The increase in the number of tenement buildings did not result from the changing role of women in the home.

26. **3** The growth of labor unions in the late 1870s was the direct result of the abuses found in the workplace including child labor, unsafe working conditions, and a twelve-hour workday. The Knights of Labor was the first major labor union formed in America. It began as a secret union with both skilled and unskilled workers as members. The Knights of Labor sought an eight-hour workday, equal pay for men and women, and the abolition of child labor. The Knights of Labor was unsuccessful in achieving its goals and was eventually replaced by the American Federation of Labor in 1881, founded by Samuel Gompers.

Wrong Choices Explained:

(1) Young children working in factories were one of the problems of the Industrial Age that led to the development of labor unions.

(2) Unsafe working conditions in the factories of the time were one of the problems that led to the development of labors unions.

(4) A twelve-hour workday was one of the problems that led to the development of labor unions.

27. **1** The economic history of the United States between 1865 to 1900 can be best described as a period in which industrialization increased at a rapid rate. This time period has been called America's "Industrial Age." It was characterized by the growth of large corporations and tactics used by business leaders like Andrew Carnegie, John D. Rockefeller, and Cornelius Vanderbilt. They formed monopolies and believed in a theory called Social Darwinism, whereby only the most profitable and, therefore, largest businesses, would survive.

Wrong Choices Explained:

(2) During this time period, most American factories used raw materials found within the United States.

(3) The period between 1865–1900 was marked by a dramatic increase in the number of immigrants, who served as a cheap source of labor and helped increase the industrial production of the country.

(4) The technological advancements inspired by the Civil War helped to boost industrial production when they were put to peacetime use.

28. **1** Corporations, stocks, and trusts are most closely connected with the rise of big business. The development of the corporate form of business, the use of stocks as a method to raise money for investment, and the formation of trusts to reduce and even eliminate competition were all connected with the rise of big business in America.

Wrong Choices Explained:

(2) Corporations, stocks, and trusts, although in some ways responsible for the development of the factory system, are more closely connected with the rise of big business.

(3) Corporations, stocks, and trusts are not as closely connected to the formation of labor unions as they are to the rise of big business.

(4) Corporations, stocks, and trusts are not as closely connected to the invention of the automobile as they are to the rise of big business.

29. **4** Manifest Destiny meant that the United States had the right to expand its borders to the Pacific Ocean. It was the nineteenth-century philosophy held by most Americans whereby they believed that it was God's will for the United States to expand its borders from the Atlantic to the Pacific. Expansion of U.S. borders during this time was accomplished through purchase as well as conquest of territory.

Wrong Choices Explained:

(1) Manifest Destiny did not mean that Native American Indians had an equal claim to the lands of the West. In fact, Native Americans were victims of Manifest Destiny, with many forced off their lands and into reservations.

(2) Manifest Destiny concerned the right of the United States to expand its borders to the Pacific Ocean. It did not involve the issue of slavery.

(3) The Monroe Doctrine, not Manifest Destiny, declared that no more European colonies would be allowed in the Americas.

30. **2** The outbreak of World War I was the result of growing nationalism, power struggles between nations, and the formation of alliances between countries. The war began in 1914 after the assassination of Archduke Franz Ferdinand by a Serbian nationalist. As a result, Germany came to the aid of its ally Austria-Hungary and Russia prepared to defend Serbia. These power struggles between nations and the entanglement of alliances resulted in declarations of war by Germany, Russia, France, and England.

Wrong Choices Explained:

(1) The growth of intense nationalism was one of the causes of World War I.

(3) Power struggles among the nations of Europe were one of the causes of World War I.

(4) The formation of alliances was one of the causes of World War I.

31. **2** Patriotic appeals were used to gain support for the Prohibition movement. The Prohibition movement, founded by the Women's Christian Temperance Union and the Anti-Saloon League, began in the United States during the 1850s and 1860s. By 1917, 26 states had passed laws prohibiting the sale and consumption of alcohol. The poster attempts to appeal to the patriotic feelings of Americans. U.S. soldiers were fighting in Europe during World War I and the poster suggests that support of Prohibition would be a sign of support for them.

Wrong Choices Explained:

(1) Prohibition was not a major goal of the United States during World War I. The main goal of the United States was to defeat the Central powers and "make the world safe for democracy."

(3) Alcohol abuse by soldiers was not a major problem for the U.S. military during World War I.

(4) Although trench warfare on the Western front did lead to large casualties, the poster was concerned with the issue of Prohibition.

32. **4** Many Americans opposed U.S. membership in the League of Nations because they feared that it would lead to involvement in another European war. The League of Nations was part of the Treaty of Versailles, which ended World War I. President Woodrow Wilson helped negotiate the treaty as part of his Fourteen Points. The United States, under the leadership of Henry Cabot Lodge, voted to reject the treaty because the Senate felt that involvement in a world organization like the League of Nations would make it more likely that the United States would again become involved in another European war.

Wrong Choices Explained:

(1) Payment of membership dues was not an issue in the debate over whether the United States should join the League of Nations.

(2) The organization of the League of Nations was based on democratic principles, including equal voting rights among member nations.

(3) The fact that Germany was allowed to join the League of Nations was not an issue in the debate over whether the United States should join the League of Nations.

33. **2** The stock market crash of 1929 is credited by many as the event that started the Great Depression. Marked by high unemployment, decreased industrial production, and numerous bank failures, the Depression lasted until the outbreak of World War II, which created a demand for war materials that put people and factories back to work.

Wrong Choices Explained:

(1) Franklin D. Roosevelt was elected president in 1932 during the height of the Great Depression.

(3) The Senate's failure to ratify the Treaty of Versailles is not credited as an event leading to the start of the Great Depression.

(4) New Deal legislation was adopted to combat the problems created by the Great Depression.

34. **4** According to the law of supply and demand, farmers will receive the highest price for their products when the supply of those products is low and the demand for them is high. According to this economic principle, when there is not enough of a product for everyone who wants to buy it, suppliers will be able to obtain the highest prices possible as those who want to purchase the product compete with one another by bidding up the price.

Wrong Choices Explained:
(1) When both supply and demand are high, prices usually remain the same.

(2) When both supply and demand are low, prices usually remain low.

(3) When supply is high and demand is low, prices are usually low.

35. **3** The New Deal is associated with the idea that the government must take responsibility for helping those in need. The legislation of the New Deal, proposed by Franklin D. Roosevelt in response to the economic problems created by the Great Depression, was based on the principle that the government must assume responsibility for the well being of its citizens when citizens are unable to care for themselves. The focus of New Deal legislation was on social welfare programs designed to provide economic relief to those in need.

Wrong Choices Explained:
(1) The New Deal is associated with the idea that government must take responsibility for helping those in need. It marked a drastic change in policy, and a retreat from Social Darwinism, which believed that the success or failure of citizens should be based on the talents and abilities of people without government interference.

(2) While churches and charities provided some relief, such as homeless shelters and soup kitchens, only the federal government had the resources necessary to provide aid on a nationwide scale.

(4) Local governments were not equipped to take care of their citizens. Only the federal government had the resources required to combat the problems caused by the Great Depression.

36. **2** The German invasion of Poland, in 1939, caused England and France to declare war on Germany. The English and French declarations of war marked the end of their policy of appeasement towards Germany.

Wrong Choices Explained:
(1) The signing of the Munich Agreement, which allowed Germany to reclaim land that it was forced to give up after World War I, was not the event leading to war. The Munich Agreement was part of a policy of appeasement, giving in to Hitler's demands in order to avoid war.
(3) Germany's alliance with the Soviet Union was not the event that caused England and France to declare war on Germany.
(4) The bombing of London occurred after war was declared, and, therefore, was not the cause of the war itself.

37. **4** The Holocaust is used to refer to the systematic murder of European Jews and other ethnic minorities by Nazi Germany during World War II.

Wrong Choices Explained:
(1) The term *appeasement* refers to the policy followed by Great Britain and other European countries prior to World War II whereby Germany was allowed to reclaim territory that it had lost after World War I along with new territory without opposition.
(2) *Blitzkrieg* refers to the German military tactic used during World War II. German for "lightning war," it is a tactic marked by rapid and massive uses of force by air and on land.
(3) *Containment* refers to the policy followed by the United States during the Cold War in an effort to stop the spread of communism.

38. **3** During the Cold War, the United States used the policy of containment to limit the spread of communism. After World War II ended, the United States pursued a policy of containment, aimed at preventing the Soviet Union from extending its influence to other countries.

Wrong Choices Explained:

(1) The U.S. policy of containment was not used to limit the spread of parliamentary democracies. This system of government, characterized by free elections and the rule of law, is the type used by Great Britain. The United States supported this type of government.

(2) The U.S. policy of containment was not used to limit the spread of absolute monarchies.

(4) Fascism, a political philosophy supported by the Nazis, had been put down during World War II, and, therefore, was not what the U.S. policy of containment sought to limit.

39. **2** One reason why many Americans opposed U.S. involvement in the war in Vietnam was that they considered it a civil war that did not concern the United States. The United States' involvement in the war began to escalate in 1964, after Congress passed the Gulf of Tonkin resolution.

Wrong Choices Explained:

(1) While many Americans did not believe that communism should be allowed to spread in Asia, they did not want the United States to get involved in the conflict in order to stop it.

(3) Americans were not opposed to U.S. involvement because they thought the conflict should be resolved by the Soviet Union.

(4) Americans were not opposed to U.S. involvement because the war was causing problems for Europe.

40. **2** The *Brown* v. *Board of Education* decision, the Montgomery bus boycott, and the March on Washington were all efforts by African-Americans to guarantee civil rights to all citizens of the United States. The end of racial discrimination and segregation were the goals that all three events helped to accomplish.

Wrong Choices Explained:

(1) These events were not efforts to protect the freedom of speech.

(3) These events were not efforts to promote economic reform.

(4) The persecution of the McCarthy Era ended prior to these events.

41. **3** The timeline best supports the statement that the right to vote has been gradually extended. The title of the timeline, "Who Could Vote

When," gives you a clue. When you look at the timeline, you should notice that in the 1780s only adult white males who owned property were allowed to vote, and that as time passed, the right to vote was extended to other groups.

Wrong Choices Explained:

(1) The use of the absolute word *all* is a clue that this is an incorrect choice. The timeline clearly indicates that only adult white males who owned property were allowed to vote early in our history and that the right to vote has gradually been extended to others over time.

(2) Although it is true that a relatively low percentage of eligible voters actually vote in national elections, the information in the timeline does not address this issue.

(4) This an opinion, rather than a fact. The information in the timeline is factual.

42. **2** The author of this statement is probably trying to point out that the attitudes of the American people are difficult to change. While women received the right to vote in 1920, it wasn't until Geraldine Ferraro's selection by presidential candidate Walter Mondale that a major political party put a woman on a national ticket. The author's statement best reflects the fact that early attitudes toward women, and the belief that women were not qualified to hold such high offices, although changing, have been slow to do so.

Wrong Choices Explained:

(1) Although allowed to seek high office, women have only recently been able to effectively do so as the attitudes of Americans have shifted, with most people believing that a woman can be qualified to run for high office.

(3) This is incorrect because there were women who expressed publicly that they would accept the nomination for president or vice president before 1984.

(4) This is incorrect because there were many women who served in Congress before 1984.

43. **3** The cartoon best illustrates the concept of imperialism. The cartoon depicts "Uncle Sam," a symbol of the United States, placing American flags onto the various overseas territories it controlled around the globe,

including Cuba, Puerto Rico, and the Philippines. This cartoon illustrates the concept of imperialism, the policy pursued by the United States in the late nineteenth and early twentieth centuries, whereby the United States sought to expand its influence around the world through control of foreign territories. One such example was the Spanish-American War, which marked the first time the United States went to war with the specific purpose of expanding its overseas possessions. As a result of the war, the United States obtained control of Cuba, Puerto Rico, the Philippines, Guam, and Hawaii.

Wrong Choices Explained:
(1) The cartoon does not illustrate the concept of secession.
(2) The cartoon does not illustrate the concept of Prohibition.
(4) The cartoon does not illustrate the concept of communism.

44. **4** Sectionalism contributed most to the start of the Civil War. Sectionalism, the development of rivalries and alliances within a country based on geographic or economic differences, created great differences between the North and South prior to the Civil War on issues like tariffs, slavery, and states' rights. After Lincoln's election in 1860, these sectional differences came to a head, resulting in the secession of Southern states.

Wrong Choices Explained:
(1) Sectionalism did not contribute to the start of the labor union movement.
(2) The stock market crash of 1929, not sectionalism, is credited for starting the Great Depression.
(3) Sectionalism did not contribute to the start of the Industrial Revolution.

45. **2** The terms *deficit spending*, *debtor nation status*, and *trade imbalance* refer to economic problems. Deficit spending occurs when a government spends more money than it receives from revenues such as taxes. *Debtor nation status* refers to the economic consequences of a country buying goods through loans with the promise to pay back the loan with interest. A *trade imbalance* refers to the economic consequences of a country's inability to sell more goods overseas than it buys from foreign countries.

Wrong Choices Explained:
   (1) These terms do not refer to social problems.
   (3) These terms do not refer to racial problems.
   (4) These terms do not refer to environmental problems.

Part II: Constructed Response Scoring Guidelines and Answers Explained

Each item consists of a single prompt or stimulus (a graph, chart, map, timeline, reading passage, and so on) on which two or more open-ended questions are based. In this model exam, there are four constructed response items. Each item has three or more questions based on it for a total of 15 questions. In general, short-answer, open-ended questions within a constructed response item are awarded credit in one of two ways. The amount of credit allocated for an individual constructed response question is determined by whether or not the item has a clear-cut answer.

One point is allocated for an individual question that has a clearly defined response and no partially correct response. The correct response is worth one credit and an incorrect response receives zero credit.

Two points are allocated when a question may elicit either a correct response (worth two credits), a partially correct response (worth one credit), or an incorrect response (worth zero credit).

To receive full credit for a response to a constructed response question, you do not have to develop your answer in a complete sentence or sentences. In addition, a correct response copied directly from a passage or paraphrased from a passage should also receive full credit.

   1. (1 point) The subject of the map is the building of the Erie Canal.

Answer Explained:
The title of the map, "Building of the Erie Canal," is your clue as to the map's subject matter. Other information contained in the map, including the course of the canal and the cities linked by it, clearly indicates that the map contains information related to the building of the Erie Canal.

   2. (1 point) The first year that goods could be shipped between Albany and Buffalo by the Erie Canal was 1825.

Answer Explained:
The map shows that Albany and Buffalo are at the opposite ends of the canal, and therefore, goods could not be shipped by the Erie Canal until its completion. The map also shows that the Erie Canal did not connect Buffalo with the rest of upstate New York until 1825. That is the first year that goods could have been shipped between the two cities by the canal.

3. (1–2 points) One major consequence of the Erie Canal was that it linked the West with the eastern part of the United States, providing an inexpensive way to ship agricultural products and lumber to market.

Answer Explained:
Any response describing the Erie Canal's impact on the economic growth of the United States would be correct. Another acceptable response would include that the building of the Erie Canal made New York City a major port for exporting farm products from the upper Midwest.

A response that does not include a description of the canal's impact on the economic growth of the United States, such as "It linked the West with the East," would result in a 1-point score.

4. (1 point) The poster is warning the "colored people of Boston."

Answer Explained:
The poster is clearly addressed to the "colored people of Boston." "Fugitive slaves" or "runaway slaves" would also be acceptable.

5. (1–2 points) These people are being warned because, under the Fugitive Slave Act, fugitive slaves were treated as "lost property" and could be captured and returned to their owners. Local watchmen and police officers were empowered to assist the slave catchers.

Answer Explained:
A correct 2-point response must explain that the poster warns the colored people of Boston that the Fugitive Slave Act considered escaped slaves as lost property and allowed watchmen and police officers to assist in their capture and return to their Southern owners. A response explaining that "colored people" could be caught would result in a 1-point score.

6. (1 point) The group most likely responsible for publishing this poster is the Abolitionists.

Answer Explained:
Abolitionists believed slavery was wrong and wanted to end it through legislation. By warning the "colored people of Boston" to beware of watchmen and police officers, Abolitionists hoped that they could prevent the return of fugitive slaves to their Southern owners and defeat the purposes of the Fugitive Slave Act.

7. (1 point) The telegram was sent by "Tozai Club of New York."

Answer Explained:
By looking at the telegram, you should notice that it is signed at the bottom by the "Tozai Club of New York." "American citizens of Japanese descent" would also be acceptable.

8. (1 point) The telegram was sent to President Franklin Roosevelt.

Answer Explained:
The telegram is addressed to "His Excellency the President of the U.S." and it is dated December 7, 1941. Based on your knowledge of social studies, you should know that Franklin Roosevelt was president at that time.

9. (1 point) The Japanese attacked Pearl Harbor on that day.

Answer Explained:
As discussed, the telegram is dated December 7, 1941. Based on your knowledge of social studies, you should know that Japan attacked the U.S. naval base at Pearl Harbor, Hawaii on that day.

10. (1 point) They were concerned because, although they were American citizens, they were of Japanese descent and did not want to be associated with Japan's attack on Pearl Harbor.

Answer Explained:
The telegram indicates that it was sent by the Tozai Club, American citizens of Japanese descent, and it condemns Japan's attack on Pearl

Harbor. Japanese-Americans had faced racial persecution and discrimination in the United States before the attack on Pearl Harbor, and they did not want to be associated with the actions of Japan.

11. (1 point) On the West Coast many Japanese were arrested by the FBI after Pearl Harbor. Loyalty hearings were conducted. Later, Japanese-Americans were confined to internment camps.

Answer Explained:
Japanese-Americans feared that they would be punished for Japan's attack on Pearl Harbor. Arrests of Japanese-Americans following the attack on Pearl Harbor were common. Eventually, American citizens of Japanese descent were relocated to internment camps due to questions about their loyalty.

12. (1 point) The Bureau of the Census.

Answer Explained:
The source for the chart is the Bureau of the Census, as indicated in the chart's source line.

13. (1–2 points) Females who are not high school graduates.

Answer Explained:
By locating the lowest average annual earnings figure and then tracing over to the "characteristic" column, and up to the level of education, the chart shows that the lowest average annual earnings, $9,311, belongs to a female who is not a high school graduate. A response of "female" or "not a high school graduate" would score 1 point.

14. (1 point) Males earned more than females.

Answer Explained:
By comparing the average annual earnings of males and females at each level of education, the chart indicates that males earned more than females at every level.

15. (1–2 points) For all groups, average earnings were higher for persons with more education.

Answer Explained:

By comparing each "characteristic" group's average annual earnings at each level of education, the chart indicates that in all groups, the average annual earnings increased as the amount of education increased. A response based on an incomplete comparison, such as "Males who were high school graduates earned more than males who were not high school graduates" would score 1 point.

Part III: Document-Based Essay—Short Answers Explained

Document 1: Illustration of a woman from the Dakota tribe preparing a buffalo hide.

1. Based on this illustration, what evidence is there that buffaloes were important to Native American Indians?

Scoring Guide

Score of 2

- Understands the importance of buffaloes to Native American Indians
- Any of the following responses is acceptable:
  Native American Indians used buffaloes for making tipis, food, and clothing.
  Native American Indians wasted no part of the buffalo.

Score of 1

- Interpretation of the illustration is limited
- Part of the response may be correct, part may be incorrect
- Response demonstrates a vague or incomplete understanding of the importance of the buffalo to Native American Indians

Score of 0

- No understanding of the illustration
- Fails to address the question
- No response

Document 2: "Crossing Over the Great Plains by Ox-Wagon."

2. According to the document, what were two reasons people wanted to "Go West"?

Scoring Guide

Score of 2

- States at least two reasons why people wanted to "Go West"
- Acceptable answers may include:
  There was fertile land in Oregon.
  The discovery of gold in California.
  The claim to 640 acres of land.

Score of 1

- Provides only one reason why people moved west
- Response is vague and lacks detail

Score of 0

- "Pioneer spirit in blood" not acceptable
- No response
- Blank paper

Document 3: A Homestead Deed.

3. According to this deed, how many acres of land did each homesteader obtain from the government under the Homestead Act?

Scoring Guide

Score of 1

- Correctly interprets the Homestead deed by stating that settlers would receive 160 acres.

Score of 0

- Does not understand the document
- Fails to address the question
- No response

Document 4: Union Pacific Railway poster.

4. Based on this poster, state two reasons people took passage on the railroad from Omaha to San Francisco.

Scoring Guide

Score of 2

- Provides two correct reasons concerning travel on the railroad
- Clearly addresses the content of the poster with answers such as:
  To visit San Francisco, to conduct business, for pleasure, health, good accommodations.
  It was safer than travel by sea.
  Train travel was the quickest way to travel to the West.

Score of 1

- Provides a partial response
- One of the stated reasons is incorrect

Score of 0

- Answers such as "four days" are too vague to receive credit
- No response

Document 5: *Illustration of a buffalo hunt.*

5a. According to this illustration, why were men killing buffalo?

Scoring Guide

Score of 1

- Clearly understands that the men on the train were killing buffalo for sport, fun, or pleasure.

Score of 0

- No understanding of the document
- No response

5b. How did this purpose for hunting differ from those of Native American Indians? (See also **Document 1.**)

Scoring Guide

Score of 2

- Clearly understands that the Native American Indians killed buffalo to stay alive. They used the entire animal, whereas the whites on the train saw the killing of buffaloes as sport. Their lifestyle did not depend on the buffalo hunt.

Score of 1

- Student understands why Native American Indians hunted the buffalo, but is unable to fully articulate the perspective of the white hunter.
- Student provides too general a response.

Score of 0

- Fails to address the question
- No response
- No understanding of the document

Document 6: Grand Rush poster.

6a. According to this poster, how many acres of former Indian territory were going to be opened for settlement?

Scoring Guide

Score of 1

- States that over 15 million acres of land are available for settlement.

Score of 0

- Fails to address question
- Response is incorrect
- No response

6b. Based on the poster, state two reasons settlers would want to move west of the Mississippi.

Scoring Guide

Score of 2

- Can clearly state two reasons why settlers would want to move west of the Mississippi

■ Possible responses might include:
Fifteen million acres of land were open for settlement.
New homes, beautiful country, timber, rich land, water.

Score of 1

■ Provides only one correct reason why settlers would want to move west of the Mississippi, or two responses were given and one was incorrect

Score of 0

■ Fails to address question
■ No response
■ Response is incorrect

Document 7: Surrender of Chief Joseph.

7. Based on this statement, state two reasons Chief Joseph finally decided to surrender to the United States government troops.

Scoring Guide

Score of 2

■ Student can clearly state two reasons why Chief Joseph surrendered to United States government troops
■ Acceptable answers include:
Chief Joseph was tired of fighting.
His chiefs had been killed.
Children were freezing to death.
His people had no blankets or food.
The Nez Perce had been scattered.

Score of 1

■ Student provides only one reason, or two responses were given and one was incorrect

Score of 0

■ No understanding of the statement
■ Fails to address the question
■ No response

Part III: Document-Based Question—Sample Student Response Essay

Based on the Specific Scoring Rubric, beginning on page 262, the sample student response essay would have received the highest score possible for this section of the test.

Throughout the history of the United States different individuals and groups have held a variety of perspectives on important issues. Easterners moving westward is one of these issues. For many Americans, the move west was a part of the Manifest destiny of the United States, but for others it meant the end of a way of life.

One event in the United State's history was when European, American, or pioneers moved westward. They decided to move westward because of the gold rush in California. Back then, everybody's dream was to be rich. This was a big opportunity to gain their dream. Also, moving westward meant equality. You could make up your own rules. You would get along with everybody. You could have your own bit of "Paradise." Nobody could boss you around or tell you what to do. Who would not want to do that?

Another big impact in the United States was the railroads on the west. Before railroads were built in the west, they were built in the North East. This made trading easier and boomed up the economy. Now having railroads in the west you could make good money. You could give your raw goods to the factories and they would pay you. Also, it would ruin the Indian's land which you would see in a little while! Instead of having open land, the land would now be full of train tracks. Also you could travel from east to west much faster then what the pioneers did. You won't have to worry about your horses dying or catching disease or be exhausted because you ride in a train for the 4 days it takes to get there and do nothing but relax.

Western expansion changed the lives of the Native Americans drastically. The Native Americans were forced to move from one place to another living in reservations while your land is being destroyed. Train tracks will take up the land and animals would just be killed for food and be left to rot while you can make lots of stuff with. Also, lots of tribes were wiped out because they weren't used to the white men's diseases. One terrible thing the white men did was they layed blankets covered with diseases on the Native American's land. When the Native Americans found those blankets, they decide not to waste them. They used them for everything. They would all die and the white men would take over the land. There were some tribes that did not let their land be taken away from them. They put on a fight. They also killed lots of Native Americans because they didn't have the rifles like we did to defend themselves. Lots of chiefs died, children froze and died. If you look at Chief Joseph of Nez Perce's surrender, you could see how tired and sick he was saying how he will fight no more forever.

In conclusion, the expansion moving westward changed the United States in a good way and in a bad way. These three examples cause a great impact for present-day America. In my opinion, even though I feel bad for the Native Americans the expansion westward not only made America bigger, it improved our economy and with the trains and railroads, it made us improve our technology.

Part III: Document Based-Question

Part B—Essay
Specific Scoring Rubric

5

- Thoroughly addresses all aspects of the Task (identifying and discussing reasons Eastern settlers moved westward, describing the impact of railroads on the West, and explaining the impact of this westward movement on the lives of Native American Indians) by accurately analyzing and interpreting at least four documents
- Places documents into a historical context by organizing documents into such groupings as reasons for moving westward, the impact of the railroad on the West, and the impact of this westward movement on Native American Indians
- Weaves information and ideas from the documents smoothly into the fabric of the essay by explaining how the movement of settlers and the building of railroads had a negative impact on the traditional lifestyles of Native American Indians
- Incorporates relevant and useful outside information such as background on the Homestead Act of 1862, a comparison of travel by railroad with travel to California by sea or wagon, the economic impact of the Union Pacific Railroad on the American economy, and the closing of the frontier

- Understands and effectively uses such key terms as frontier, economic expansion, pioneers, and manifest destiny
- Richly supports essay with relevant facts and examples such as details of the Gold Rush, life on the Oregon Trail, and the traditional lifestyle of the Plains Indians
- Shows an ability to discuss, describe, and explain the westward movement from the perspectives of settlers, Native American Indians, and the railroads
- Writes a well-organized essay demonstrating a clear and logical plan of organization, with a balance of facts and analysis of the documents worked smoothly into the essay
- Introduces the Task with a framework that is beyond a simple restatement of the Task and concludes with a solid summary

4

- Addresses all aspects of the Task (identifying and discussing reasons settlers moved westward, describing the impact of railroads on the West, and explaining the impact of this westward movement on the lives of Native American Indians) by accurately analyzing and interpreting at least four documents
- Places documents into historical context by grouping the documents
- Incorporates relevant and useful outside information such as background information on the Homestead Act of 1862, a comparison of travel by railroad with travel to California by sea or wagon, the economic impact of the Union Pacific Railroad on the American economy, and the closing of the frontier
- Understands and effectively uses such key terms as frontier, economic expansion, pioneers, and manifest destiny
- Supports essay with relevant facts and examples in their proper historical context or setting, but the discussion may be more descriptive than analytical; for example, does not fully discuss the impact of railroads on the West
- Shows an ability to discuss, describe, and explain the westward movement without the rich and full detail of a "5" answer
- Writes a well-organized essay demonstrating a clear and logical plan of organization; facts and analysis of the documents may be worked unevenly into the body of the essay

- Introduces the Task with a framework that is beyond a simple restatement of the Task and concludes with a solid summary

3

- Understands and addresses some aspects of the Task, or all aspects in a limited way by identifying and discussing some reasons settlers moved westward, describing the impact of railroads on the West, and explaining the impact of this westward movement on the lives of Native American Indians, and interpreting and using three of the documents
- Identifies and uses some relevant documents, incorporating them into the body of the essay
- Places some (but not all) documents into a historical context
- Incorporates little relevant and useful outside information, such as the context of the Homestead Act or the details regarding the impact of the Union Pacific Railroad on the United States
- Understands and uses some key terms, such as frontier, pioneers
- Supports essay with some relevant facts and examples in their proper historical context or setting, but the discussion is superficial
- Shows an ability to discuss, describe, and explain the westward movement, but in a limited way and not in depth
- Writes a satisfactory essay demonstrating a general plan of organization with facts and description of the documents worked somewhat unevenly into the body of the essay
- Introduces the Task by repeating the Task or Historical Context (a simple restatement of the Task) and concludes by simply repeating the Task or Historical Context

2

- Attempts to address some aspects of the Task (identifying and discussing vague reasons why Eastern settlers moved westward, possibly describing the impact of railroads on the West, and explaining the impact of this westward movement on the lives of Native American Indians) but with little use of the documents
- Includes few facts, examples, and details of the westward movement; discussion only paraphrases the contents of documents
- Incorporates no relevant and useful outside information

- Uses key terms such as pioneer or frontier, but in a vague or incorrect manner
- Writes a poor essay, demonstrating a poor plan of organization, responding to only some parts of the Task; lacks focus
- Fails to introduce or summarize westward movement

1

- Shows very limited understanding of the Task, with unclear or no references to the documents
- Presents no relevant outside information about the westward movement
- Includes little or no accurate or relevant facts, details, or examples
- Understanding and use of key terms such as frontier or pioneer is vague or incorrect
- Writes a poor essay, demonstrating a major weakness in organization; lacks focus
- Has vague or inadequate introduction and conclusion

0

- Fails to address the Task, is illegible, or is a blank paper